Old C

In the early days of the century an ~~occasional~~ broadsheet used to circulate around the village. In it 'Old Crow' used to award a 'putty medal' to locals who had done something special. Ted the Post remembers some of the awards. To:

George who lifted his pig on to the top of the wall to watch a performance by the Crich United Silver Prize Band.

Olive who put barm in her rice pudding.

Lily A who starched her silk stockings.

Lily S who cut a currant in half to make up the weight.

Crowie who thatched his stack from the top.

George D, the poacher, who had a standing weekly order for two rabbits from Sergeant W at the Police House.

Mrs Tom T for making a pasty without cutting the rhubarb up. Half of it was in the oven: half rested on a stool in the hearth.

P.C. B. who, when asked by Pot Jack if the King's Arms was open, said 'Why — are they ever shut?'

Rings who enquired of the goings-on of his wife by saying 'Asta sayn mi bag o bones?'

Specky who carried a wall clock from Coddington to Crich Church to get the correct time.

Jack who went into Bradley's shop and asked for a motor-bike cap. 'Wonn wi a brim at t'back'.

He who repeats a tale after a man
Is bound to say, as nearly as he can,
Each single word, if he remembers it,
However rudely spoken or unfit
Or else the tale he tells will be untrue . . .

Geoffrey Chaucer
Prologue to the Canterbury Tales
Neville Coghill Translation

Phototypesetting and artwork by Prior to Print, 44 Friar Gate, Derby
Printed by Heanor Gate Printing Limited, Heanor, Derbyshire
© J. G. Dawes 1983
ISBN 0 907758 06 1

Acknowledgements

Most builders of monuments use parts made by others —
and sometimes things that have been used before.
In setting down these stories it has been a delight to have
the help of many friends.
I want especially to thank the following, without whom this
book would not have been possible:
my brother Peter, Denis Else, Trudy Gill, Ted Rollinson
and Les Rollinson.
All these would, I'm sure, like to join me in saluting
Eva Ashley, who is no longer with us, but who should really
have the credit for the collection.
I am also indebted to, and thank,
Dave Mitchell and George Power for useful comment and
help in slimming down and re-arranging my
original material.

J.G.D.

*The publishers are grateful to Penguin Books for permission to quote from
the prologue to 'The Canterbury Tales', Neville Coghill translation*

The Crich Tales

Unexpurgated Echoes from a Derbyshire Village

Collected and set down by
Geoffrey Dawes

Illustrations by Geoff Taylor

Published 1983 by Scarthin Books
Cromford, Derbyshire

Prologue

Crich is now quite well-known: if there is a tram-car on film or the television screen it is quite likely that the shooting was done there — with the track on a bed laid by George Stephenson.

The village rests on one of the south-eastern foothills of the Pennines, in mid Derbyshire. The name, Crich, comes from the Celtic language of the ancient Britons, and means, simply, 'Hill'.

Records about the place have been made for at least eight hundred years but, in the last few generations, in the change from candle-light, privvies and the pony and trap to frozen foods and video recorders, the village has lost much of its self-sufficiency. Talk has become more and more moulded to BBC standards and there seem to be fewer personalities about.

To try and preserve some of the atmosphere and fun of the comparatively recent past this collection presents yarns and sayings (many woven into their everyday speech) known to a particular family and its friends and told about local people: some present but mostly gone. To say, for instance, 'Is it way' to them conveys a whole paragraph of meaning.

Most of the stories are 'true' but, without doubt, some are told about local characters even though they originated in 'public-house music-halls' or are traditional.

At some pages, if you're not a Tup, you may have to puzzle the meaning out; but you may enjoy doing that — and if not, there is a glossary at the back of the book which will help.

The Order of the Tales

Hewers' Tales

Millstones from Crich are mentioned in the fourteenth century *Rolls of Barlow Manor*, near Sheffield; and for at least two hundred years the villagers have had the right, granted by the Hurt family of Alderwasley, to take stone for their own use from the Tors Quarry. Hardwick Hall Accounts for 1596 include 'one horse load of Crich lyme to whyte with', and it is for limestone quarrying that the village is renowned. In the eighteenth century the Butterley Company had a gangway carrying limestone from a quarry off the Dimple Valley, down to kilns near the canal at Bullbridge; but the largest quarry, at Crich Cliff, was developed by Stephenson's Clay Cross Company in the 1840's.

In its heyday the Cliff Quarry employed 120 men. The work was skilled and dangerous. The quarrymen had to reach their section of the cliff face using chains and ropes; then, working in small teams, using sledgehammers and bars, they drilled holes to take the black powder explosive. The broken stone was taken in wagons down to the kilns at Ambergate along a track which went through a tunnel under Sandy Lane. The Cliff Quarry was closed in 1957, and the familiar sound of everyone's favourite engine Dowie and the boom of blasting were not heard again. The bed of Cliff Quarry is now home to the National Tramway Museum.

Leadmining was developed by the Romans, and it provided great wealth in the Liberty of Crich in medieval times. Its monument is the present parish church; but by the end of the nineteenth century there were few lead-miners left, and even they were more concerned with winning fluorspar.

In the first half of the present century many coal-miners, mostly working at Oakerthorpe Colliery, lived in the village. They and the quarrymen did much to give Crich its unique flavour over a period covering the lives of grandfathers and fathers and their sons, who are the grandfathers of today. It is with tales of these tough men that we begin.

Fred — nicknamed Pot Jack — was one of the rough and tough quarrymen who laboured on Crich Cliff, and he had a running vendetta with Captain B the Quarry Manager. Pot had served in the 14-18 War in the 'Foresters' under Brigadier J. If he had a real up-and-downer with Captain B and wasn't satisfied, he'd walk the 7 miles or so to Clay Cross to the Hall, and tell his tale to Mrs J (who he claimed, often gave him half-a-crown for past-rendered services!) She'd take Pot to see his 'Boofull General'. After a telephone call from Clay Cross to Crich he'd often walk back with a note from the Brigadier to Captain B sorting out the trouble

*   *   *   *   *

Some of the men from the Cliff Quarry occasionally organised a 'pink-pyjama' day. They used to forgather at opening time and drink through until they were broke, or were turned out, or went to sleep. Before then they usually got around to singing of the lady who came round the mountain in pyjamas — presumably of pink silk. After one such day Pot turned up at the quarry to meet the irate Captain B, who said he'd had enough and gave Pot his cards, 'and if you try to go on the dole, I'll stop that!'

'If yew deow, mester, t'sargery bell'll deow a lot o' knollin,' was the response.

*   *   *   *   *

In winter, Crich Cliff was a cold place to work. One year, when the Church Jumble Sale was held, Harriet, Pot's wife, had a bit of money to spare and bought him a pair of long-johns. Pot had never worn underwear before. When he came down from the privvy up the garden he was in quite a mess, and admitted he hadn't taken his pants down with his trousers. As he said:

'So thet's it — ar thowt theer wer nowt droppin.'

*   *   *   *   *

Harriet walked into the tap-room at the King's Arms to see Pot Jack with his 'tackle' out and resting on the table.

'Wot dusta think thay't on wi?'

'Ar'm shewin' 'em owd Noah fer a pint fer may', says Pot. So Harriet picks up her clouts and declares:

'Thay can say 'is ark fer annutha pint.'

9

When Pot gave Harriet a pound note for her weekly housekeeping she held it up and blew on the edge. Pot declared:
'Thay needna bother — theer's non likely ter be no more ne wonn.'

* * * * *

Some remembered remarks of Pot Jack:
'Mi missus allus gies may an egg fer mi breakfast: sumtimes tew — but nivva ne less ne wonn.'

'Ower Charlie? Arr: it's appendicitis agen: an ays 'ad tew-thray opperations fer that awreddi.'
(Waxing musical) 'Tic-a-ta, tic-a-ta, tic-a tom, ta-ta'. 'That's black-note moosic. Mi bruther used ter play it ont' euphonium — but ay got 'is 'ead shot-off at Mons an that stopped 'is euphonium playin.'
'Mi wife's nowt but a mucky wumman. Evvritime ar gew fer a piss in t'slopstewn it's full er dotti pots.'
And after Harriet had died:
'Arr, ower 'Arriet is gone. It wer t'trembollis as got 'er: Ar cudna persayve 'er in t'choch yard: but ar can allus say 'er in t'chamber!'

* * * * *

Clarence and Herbert, owned and ran a licensed coal mine. In the Comrades' Club, before a Tombola session, Clarence remarked:
'Ower 'Erbert — ar'm thinkin' a changin' mi car. Ar'm gewin dahn ter Derby ter get missen wonn o them new Vanden Plush Westminsters.' Herbert replied:
'Rayht — shotta get may wonn anor, yewth!'

* * * * *

Cammy, who was about 11 to the dozen, was left at the pit bottom at Oakerthorpe Colliery to take messages. The Undermanager rang down and said 'Cammy'. 'Ar'. 'Send up a dozen tubs as sewn as yew can.' Silence. The Undermanager repeated his message — still silence. 'Cammy!!' Silence. Ring, shout, and storm as he would there was no reply. Eventually the tubs came up and at the end of the shift the Undermanager was waiting for Cammy as he came out of the lamp room. 'Yew ignorant bugger — why didna yew answer — ar't dumb?' Cammy was quite hurt. 'But ar did; ar nodded me 'ead evvri time yew towd may owt.'

Gowder was in his garden at the side of the Parks Lane one Sunday morning when a pal dropped by, admired his potatoes, and asked what kind they were, he said:
'Oakerthorpe Colliery Deputy Specials: last dahn; fost up!'

* * * * *

At snap-time on Number Eights at Oakerthorpe Colliery they were discussing buying presents for wives. Bob reckoned it was a dodgy business. 'Mi missus wannted wonn o' them brassieres an ar went inter Ripley ter Rowells and asked fer wonn — gift wrapped. T'lass sed 'wot cup size?' Ar didn'a know. Ew said: 'Well, it is egg or orange or melon big?' Got may rayht flummoxed. As ar sed ar'd more a mind on a pair a bludhernds' ears!'

* * * * *

George was going to work one morning about 6 o'clock passing the Rising Sun when there was a knock on the tap-room window and Peelock, who was already in action, beckoned him in. Peelock says: 'Ar've hayf-a-crahn'. So they supped the ten pints. George then says: 'Wot are way gewin ter deow nar — its non woth gewin ter wok'. Peelock says: 'Owd on, George: Patty'll bay gewin' aht sewn an ar know wheer ew kayps t'rent — then way can stop till dinner time'.

* * * * *

Peelock was going to Ripley and Patty asked him to bring back a meat plate for a present for her niece's wedding. He arrived home with a real beauty — about two foot six inches long by eighteen inches wide.
'Wot on earth's that thing — its far tew big: yew cud put a whole pig on it.'
'Orr-rayht', said Peelock, throwing the plate on to the stone flags on the kitchen floor: 'Pick a bit aert a thet lot thet's t'rayht size.'

* * * * *

Crusses was well endowed and of unusual, lipped, shape. This was revealed one day as he relieved himself in the quarry — when one of his mates remarked: 'Ay'd fetch more dahn than ay'd put up.'

Johnny was arranging a meeting with his workmate. He says: 'If thay't theer fost, put a stewn on t'war. Ef ar'm theer fost, ar'll knock it off.'

* * * * *

Sam rarely washed. He really was quite filthy. Once when he was ill and had to go and see the Doctor his brother took him in hand, put him in the bath, and scrubbed him. As he said: 'That's t'fost time ay's bin properly weshed sin t'midwife bathed 'im.' Once, at work, he was standing in the toilets next to an American Negro who'd stayed in England after the '39-'45 War and glanced over. The Yank said: 'Well, man, yo got one as big?' Sam said: 'Nay, lad — but ar've got wonn er t'same colour!'

* * * * *

At the time of the 1930's Depression, when many were laid-off work, the Reverend Ord walked past Arthur, who was trimming his hedge, and said: 'Good Morning.' He was greeted with the remark: 'Ellow, Vicar, ar't thay still on a wonn dee a wik, then!'

* * * * *

Walter, Wammy, was one of the tallest and strongest men in the village and he had a very varied 'career' — including the Grenadier Guards. During the '14-'18 war he was taken prisoner and spent much of it on a farm in Saxony. He didn't grumble too much, he said, because the farmer was on the Western Front and he had, perforce, as the only human male available, to deal with all sorts of 'jobs' on the farm — and this made him quite content.

* * * * *

He was demobbed early and joined the police force at Chesterfield as a constable.

With a coppers' helmet on top of six-foot-six or so Wammy really was an impressive figure and he usually attracted respect. Once he was sent to investigate a report of a man playing the devil and frightening his family and neighbours. He knocked at the door which was opened by the man wielding a butcher's cleaver. He glared at Wammy and eventually growled: 'Wot dust thay wannt?' Wammy afterwards admitted to wiping his handkerchief over the sweat of his face and, turning his head, saying 'Nuthink!' But eventually he sorted it all out.

On his beat through Chesterfield Bus Station Wammy spotted Joe — his school pal from Crich — looking grumpily at a bus that was full and on which he couldn't get. Wammy thought for a moment and then called all the passengers off the bus, put Joe on, and then said to the others: 'Yew can get back on nar — that bloke's got fother ter gew than enni er yew.'

*　*　*　*　*

When he came back to Crich, and on and off until it closed, Wammy was a quarryman on Crich Cliff. Life on the quarry face, especially in winter, was not easy and now and then he would get fed up and think it time to get a different job. What he did was to load an enormous stone on to a waggon such that when it got down to the Lime Kilns at Ambergate no single man could get it out of the waggon. There was no room for more than one to work at a time and it had to be broken up inside the waggon. This was a nuisance and did damage. Wammy's cards would then be sent back with 'Dowie's' driver and he'd be off to his new job. But he always got his job back at the Cliff face when he wanted it.

*　*　*　*　*

At a time when Alfred was the village rate-collector and was delivering demand notices Wammy saw him coming up the path and as Alfred pushed the envelope under the door Wammy wafted it out with a folded newspaper. Alfred tried again and again the demand notice was blown back out. Alfred mused: 'Don't know if I'd want to pay rates on a house as draughty as that!'

*　*　*　*　*

Wammy worked at Rolls Royce in the '39-'45 War and afterwards for the Council on the 'Lavender Waggon'. In his later years he often teamed-up with short little Luke and they used to blacken their faces and go 'guyserin' at New Year Time. Wammy's rendering of 'Burlington Bertie' was widely renowned and his trick of swallowing a mouthful of meths, breathing it out and lighting it, to put on a fire-eating act, impressed all the youngsters of a generation.

Joe — Cocky, who lived in the Dimple Hollow, was a horny-handed lead miner of wide experience and he was sent by the Butterley Company to give evidence at a court case in London. He'd never been south of the Trent before and, to look after him, the company sent along one of their young, up and coming, managers. The night before the case Cocky was missing. There was something of a panic but eventually he was discovered in the basement of the Hotel — in the barber's shop. The hairdresser was studying his head and was heard to say: 'And who usually cuts your hair, sir?' Cocky's reply was: 'Mi missus — ew usually gets a rasp ter it!'

* * * * *

One special year Cocky went to 'Weaver to Wearer' for a 35 bob suit — as advertised — and refusing to spend more, because that's what the advert had said, insisted on a 35 shilling model. The coat was a bit loose and the trousers a bit tight — but it did for Joe. That is until one Sunday when he took Mrs C a walk around Culland Wood and got caught in a thunder downpour. The coat became a firm fit — but the trousers!! Joe went back to the shop and complained. The salesman said 'Why can't you let your braces down a bit?' 'Becoss' said Joe 'it's tew bluddi uncomfortable sittin on't buttons at t'back.'

* * * * *

Gilbert was a lifetime bachelor: tall, strong — a colliery blacksmith in his prime — and, before it was demolished, he lived in a small cottage across from the Church. His cottage was furnished with orange boxes, packing cases and his coffin (made specially by Guddy and tested for size in the tap-room of the Dutchman). Gilbert slept in the coffin.

* * * * *

In his apprentice days he acted as striker for blacksmith Charlie when they were making some fancy iron work for Sam B's posh house on the Common. Charlie had heated the iron and called 'Wonn layht' but Gilbert was heavy-handed and his blow flattened the piece. In disgust Charlie swung his tongs and flung the hot iron through the window of the smithy, past the Cross, and it landed-up just in front of the Dutchman. Gilbert — with a heave — picked up the anvil and, walking outside, said 'Ar didna know as tha wannted ter wok aertside!'

15

Gilbert had odd tastes. James Henry, the grocer, used to save rancid bacon ends and sour cheese for him and kept his supply of thick-twist tobacco in a damp cellar until it acquired a green mould. He was seen to sit on the seats under trees on the Market Place, open a vein, run his blood into a saucer and carry it to the steps of the Baptist Chapel where he drank it as at his own communion. He would go to the chemist, buy a tin of Rodine Rat Killer, and eat it with his fingers, foaming at the mouth. He used to get roaring drunk, put on an army blue and scarlet dress uniform, and rampage down the village waving a cavalry sword and chasing small boys — who fled in terror. He once broke an ankle but never went near a doctor: he let it mend on its own and afterwards always walked with a bent foot and a limp.

*　*　*　*　*

Not everyone was scared of him. When the roads were being tarred for the first time the County Council had a big stock of barrels at the back of the troughs on the Market Place. Gilbert and Walter (from Holloway, who was slightly odd — or 'handicapped' as they say now-a-days) used to stalk one another amongst them. Jack, who was the engine-driver at Oakerthorpe Colliery, and had been in the 'Foresters' in the '14-'18 war, decided, one day, to join in. Gilbert spotted him and made a tremendous swipe at him with his stick. But Jack had learned well in the trenches: he parried the blow with his own staff, and then succeeded in knocking Gilbert unconscious — as he said 'Ter taych th' silly sod a lesson.'

*　*　*　*　*

One day as Ted the Post and Luke were returning from the 'Comrades Club' past Peter Percy's butchers' shop they saw Gilbert had pinned Irene into a corner of the shop, behind half a heifer hanging there, and was stroking two butcher's knives around her throat. Luke, though small, was able to disarm him and to hustle him out of the shop. He went off like a lamb.

*　*　*　*　*

Gilbert had an exhaustive knowledge of the Bible. He would quote, reliably, for hours on end. He had a vendetta with the Church, though, and especially with K the sexton and verger. He particularly disliked the bells and on one occasion he chased K with a 10 lb hammer — threatening to smash them. K managed to get into the bell tower and hold the door from inside — to keep Gilbert out: but it was a near thing. He once appeared in church at a Thursday evening choir practice and shouted 'Bugger, bugger, bugger — and that's blasphemy!' to the astonished choir boys. Often he would dress up in women's white clothes (his mother's wedding dress it was said) and go and lie amongst the graves at night. One famous Sunday morning, with nothing on but a night shirt and with all his nether parts exposed, he crawled on his hands and knees up the path to the Church porch in front of the assembling congregation. On occasion he would roar around the church yard sticking his sword into graves and shouting: 'Get up, you buggers!.'

His star turn was to hold his own private, but loudly declaimed, prayer session in the Church porch whilst Vicar Hubert E. was preaching a sermon inside.

* * * * *

The last tale about Gilbert comes from the time when he'd left Crich and lived near Matlock in a caravan not far from the 'Thorn Tree Inn'. He'd grown an enormous beard and went, one day, into the tap-room with a chamber - pot which he put down on the bar saying nothing but staring at the daughter of the house, home from college for the holiday, who was acting as barmaid. She ran, scared to death, to her mother in the kitchen. 'It's alright dear', said Mum, 'Its only Mr P. He's a regular customer now. Put a quart of bitter in the pot. He'll pay alright. He's quite harmless.' And in truth, Gilbert never, ever, hurt anyone.

Farmers' Tales

Crich has long been in a cattle and sheep rearing area, and its fairs were already well established by 1770. The cattle fairs held between the Cross and the Church attracted farmers, drovers and packmen from miles around, but the advent of the railways and then the cattle lorry caused a decline, and the fairs ended in the Twenties. The Crich commoners lost their rights of grazing after the Enclosure Awards of 1784, but many of them retained a connection with farming. There were pigstyes at many cottages before the First World War; and even as late as the Twenties there were breeding sows at a number of houses around Prospect Terrace and off Bennett's Lane.

Over the last hundred years the local farmers, working on high, exposed ground, have tended to raise sheep and calves for fattening in lusher pastures, and there are men still living who tell of their journeys driving a herd of cattle or a flock of sheep to the good grass of Chatsworth Park, some twelve to fifteen miles over Dethick Common and Middle and Beeley Moors.

Crich farmers also supplied dairy products for the local community. Some from the Culland Park area used to go to Derby Market by pony and trap with butter and eggs each week. Up to the Thirties farming provided some regular and many seasonal jobs; but farming has changed and the local farmers, who are themselves relatively prosperous, today provide little employment for others. There is now no real sense of Crich being the centre of a farming community.

George, Puddin, farmed, delivered coal, and was small, round and aware of his own importance. He was a 'regular' at the King's Arms and after a whole day there on the binge was very loth to go home. Eva, trying to get him out, said: 'You'd better get off and see to the cows.' Puddin's answer, as he drew himself up to his full five-foot-two, was: 'Ar've fed them cerws, an ar've watted them cerws. Thay'n pissed an farted an shit an thay'm hivva sew content.'

* * * * *

Puddin was telling the Tap Room about his daughter Mary's new Easter Bonnet.
'Han yer sayn ower Mary's bonnet? It's a stunna an no mistek. It's gorra bunch a roses on it an a featha dahn't back. Nar ower Mary went ter choch last Sundi an t' parson cudna find 'is text fer lewkin; an fat owd Mrs B sed: 'Why Mary, wot evva next!' After t' service t' Parson sed, most kindly, 'Mary, if tha wannts ter find thi way t'glory thay murrna wear a whole conservatory on thi 'ed.' Nar ower Mary isna short er pluck. Ew jumped round in a minnit an ew lewked as if ew'd swallad t'choch an orr t'folk in it an ew says ter t'parson. 'Thi yed's bowd: nowt on it an nowt in it. Why dunta wear a bunch a roses on it — like them in mi owd bonnet?'

* * * * *

When Donald heard George command:
'Lewk at th' magnificent harse hon her!' he took a quick look at his wife, Shiela, and then realised that Puddin was talking about the mare he was backing up the yard with the coal cart.

* * * * *

Puddin and Tom had been to the Cattle Market held just above the Cross and against the Dutchman croft wall. They had done well and they celebrated at the Dutchman and then at the Swan and then at the Sun and they arrived, happily, at the King's Arms — swearing eternal friendship. 'Tha knows, Tom, ef ar ad tew cerws, ar'd gie thi wonn.' 'Ar know tha wud Puddin.' 'An ef tha 'ad tew pigs thay'd gie may wonn, wunnta, Tom?' 'Owd on a bit, Puddin, tha knows ar've got tew pigs.'

Joe was short of cow-hair to finish-off some plastering. So he send old Will to Tiny B's farm to get a new supply. Instead of combing some of their backs Will cut off the ends of the tails of about 30 cows.

* * * * *

Dennis went across the allotments to Peter to ask him where he could relieve himself. He was directed to the top side of Frank's blackcurrants under the wall. He came back covered up to the knees with black slime and simply said:

'Peter, yew neglected ter tell may abaht that owd sough frum Martins' pig stye.'

* * * * *

Mary and Alice lived at Shuckstone Farm. They had a stallion which they used at stud — usually with Alice looking after operations. Job took his mare to be served. 'Alice 'as gon aert', says Mary. Job pleaded: 'Canna yew deow it — ar dunna wannt ter cum back agen'. 'Ar'll try', says Mary, and led the stallion out. He was just about to make his leap when Alice arrived back and, coming round the corner and knowing that Mary was strange to the job, yelled out: 'Bottom 'ole ower Mary.'

* * * * *

Tom C, after a long cold day on the tractor came into the farm kitchen where his wife was sitting by the fire knitting. He asked if his dinner was ready.

'Got yer dinna reddi! Wot deow yew think ar am!! Theer yew've bin swing-dinglin arahnd on a tractor sin dawn an 'ere ar've bin knittin' mi fingers ter th' bone and yew expect may to deow th' cookin' as well!'

* * * * *

Reginald William was told by his wife that his sister-in-law had died, that the funeral was to be on the following Thursday and they were expected to be there.

'Tha knows ar canna gew. Ar allus gew shootin' up Newhaven of a Thosdi — an enni-ow ew didna cum ter thi mutha's funeral.'

Brick and his pal were walking home from Ripley Market over Pentrich Common: they were somewhat tipsy and in a boastful mood. 'Ar've got poffect eyesight: ar can say a gnat on Crich Stand can'st thay?' 'Arr' said Brick 'That's nowt: canst thay say its eyelashes?'

* * * * *

Garner Lane at parkhead used to be very narrow — just wide enough to take a horse and cart. One day the Council Road Foreman saw Brick digging at the side of the cutting.

'Wot dusta think tha's deowin,' said the foreman. 'Who's towd thi ter d'that?'

'Nubbdi,' says Brick. 'But ar've got ter bay able ter get mi onions threw ter t'Dutchman shew!'

* * * * *

Tommy, who ran a biggish farm and owned quite a lot of property in Fritchley was notorious for his meanness. It was said that he had long pockets but only short arms. He painted the outside of his rented property himself. One day he was doing the upstairs windows at a cottage backing on to Fritchley Lane when the ladder slipped and he fell, rather heavily, to the ground, with the ladder on top of him. Grandma T ran out anxiously 'Art thay orr-rayht, Mester B?' she called. 'Thay nivva mind abaht may — ave ar spilt enni paynt?'

* * * * *

Theo was off colour and he asked Les to take a message to Tommy. It was dark when Les arrived at the farmhouse and Tommy came to the door carrying a candle, asked his business, and invited him into the parlour where there was a fire. As they sat down Tommy blew out the candle saying:

'Theers enuff layt from t'fire ter talk be — neow nayd ter waste a candle!'

* * * * *

Theo was about the only friend Tommy had, and from his privileged position, he urged Tommy not to be so miserly. He reminded Tommy that he couldn't 'take it with him' and that when he died his nephews and nieces would have a high old time spending, like water pouring away, the money that Tommy had so carefully saved. Tommy declared:

'Ef thay aay as much pleshure spendin' it as ar've ad savin' it, ar'll non grumble!'

23

Widdy had done a deal with Tommy on a bit of land at the back of Culland Wood. Widdy arrived to pay the agreed price of £300 with a stone jam-jar containing sovereigns. Tommy counted and made it 500 'Dammit,' said Widdy, 'Ew muṣt a got it off er t'wrong shelf.'

* * * * *

Theo of Church Farm at Fritchley didn't mind if children of one or two of his neighbours — who helped him out at haymaking time — played in his orchard. But, inevitably, every now and then a gang of them would rampage and annoy him. He would then chase them with his horsewhip, shouting:
'Gerroff yew lot — wonn er yor sort's plenty together!'

* * * * *

Charlie D's slaughter house was up a field from the Common and one day the drains got blocked. He put rods down and got a stop about 30 yards down the hill from the grid. He measured out from there with the rods and started digging. By now it was raining hard and going dark, and water and muck filled the bottom of the hole. Eventually he came across a clay pipe which he broke and fumbled inside. Sure enough there was a blockage — but he couldn't shift it. So he backed his lorry down to the hole and, under mud and water, fastened a wire rope around the obstruction, attached it to the tow bar on the lorry and started, gently, to drive away. After tremendous strain and a mighty jerk the lorry moved forward dragging with it the severed end of the Ashbourne telephone cable.

* * * * *

Charlie, the blacksmith, whose forge was at the Cross also ran a farm near the Church. When he was sober he was a natural gentleman but --! He came home at midnight, just as his wife's cuckoo clock was performing. He grabbed his 12-bore shot gun and blasted the bird.
'That'll kayp thi quiet tha nosey little bugger' he said.

* * * * *

Once Charlie offered Ferdin a lift on his horse and legged him over the side — right over.
'Asta fell off Ferdin?' says Charlie.
'Neow' says Ferdin 'Ar worna on.'

Jim was full of good works — and bad language. When a cow fell into the top of the shaft of an old lead mine at the back of Crich Cliff the Police, the Fire Brigade, and the cow's owner had given up hope of pulling the animal out and were about to shoot it when Jim arrived. He dug a channel into the lip of the shaft and then grabbed a hay-fork and clambered down on the collapsed capping beside the cow. By applying the fork judiciously and addressing the cow firmly he got it to see how preferable it would be to be on firm ground. With something of a struggle it clambered out itself. Jim kept the RSPCA certificate of commendation for kindness to animals over the mantlepiece in his farm-house kitchen.

Scholars' Tales

It is known that there was a Crich School in 1805, but the pattern of elementary education in Crich was not established until the Church of England Parochial School (The Top School) was opened in 1848 and the British School (the Bottom School) in 1885. Rivalry between the two schools was intense. Thus whenever there was snow on the ground it was the signal for a snowball battle, in which the girls were contestants as fierce as the boys. One girl ring-leader from the Bottom School, later a well-known and respected leader in the community, suffered the indignity of having her knickers stuffed with snow by the football hero of the Top School!

Both these schools kept their pupils until they were fourteen years old, but a few won secondary education for themselves.

After about 1910 pupils competed for free places at the Herbert Strutt School, Belper, and one or two were successful each year. Between 1920 and 1945, from a total village population of about 3,000, Crich pupils at Strutts won fifteen university scholarships. Two became Cambridge Wranglers; another became a University Vice-Chancellor; and two more became Professors; all these, interestingly, in mathematical and scientific subjects.

With the advent of comprehensive education Crich secondary pupils have been 'bussed' to Alfreton. This has certainly given adolescents a centre of interest away from their homes, but it has also spoiled, it seems, the corporate spirit that generated team and club activity within the village itself.

Harry — Skimps — was known for his 'goster' and as a lad was always in trouble. One of the many things he got away with was to drill a hole in the window front of Mrs F's shop, across from the Church, and, with a wire, recover enough aniseed balls to satisfy himself and his pals.

*   *   *   *   *

The narrow-boat was tied-up in the lock at Robin Hood and boatman Prince's wife had put a pie on the cabin roof to cool. To Skimps this was a marvellous target and he cobbed a stone at it and knocked it into the canal. Prince saw this and roared: 'If evva ar get ashore, yew young devil, ar'll brek thi bluddi neck!'

*   *   *   *   *

Skimps and his pals waged war, usually successfully, on Sergeant W. One battle started when they put a blue sugar bag filled with fresh cow dung under the oil-light at the top of the old 'Sun Steps'. The Sergeant, on his evening round, spotted it and was suspicious. After a lot of hesitation he picked it up and was fumblingly opening it when Skimps gostered. The Sergeant's hand slipped and his fingers went into the dung. With a roar he gave chase across the top of Dimple Green, round Candlehouse End, behind the Troughs, across the Market Place down School Lane and into Peter Percy's farm yard — into real darkness. Skimps and his pals, who knew their way about, divided around the muck-heap but Sergeant W went blundering on, up to his knees in manure, as Skimps gostered again, out of reach, safe.

*   *   *   *   *

Sergeant W beat Skimps on one occasion. Outside the Bull's Head he caught Skimps tying a thunderflash under the tail of one of the horses on the brewery delivery cart. Skimps was hauled before the Bench at Alfreton and, in the event, was fined. When taking the case the magistrate demanded to know if the horse had shied. Skimps response was: 'No it didna — but it wud a dun if that nosey owd bugger hadna interfered.'

Miss A was a very strict teacher. She came into class one morning sniffing the air like a peke. 'Which of you boys wants to leave the room?' (Girls, of course, were sweet!) She glared at Tom. 'It's non may' says Tom. 'It's Clem theer — ay smells like ay's shit hissen.'

'No Miss,' sobs Clem, 'It's non may — it's me new corduroy pants.' In those days corduroys had an atomosphere all of their own — especially if you'd walked through rain in them.

*　*　*　*　*

Miss A was retiring after about 30 years teaching at the Bottom School. She was popular and a collection had bought a handsome ˙present. This was given to her at a village meeting by Nosey, who was Chairman of Şchool Managers and of the Parish Council and of anything else going. With a tear in his eye he declared:

'It makes my heart bleed to see Miss A leaving because I have had very pleasant connections regularly with her for years and I am going to miss her greatly.'

*　*　*　*　*

Pete, the teacher, went up to the surgery with a sore throat. There, for the first time, he saw the new, young, and rather glamorous lady doctor. As he said:

'My illness dropped two feet straight away.'

*　*　*　*　*

Both Pete and his daughter were bell-ringers and regularly they rang on Sunday mornings — often after Pete had been partying on Saturday night. And Pete could really look terrible. The Bell-Captain, Peter who was about 20 years older than Pete often said: 'For goodness sake, Pete, don't give up ringing, so long as you can keep coming on Sunday mornings, the rest of us will feel young.'

*　*　*　*　*

Pete and his headmaster colleague Harold, on an educational project, went to visit a new Junior School in the County. It was open plan and very 'modern'. Not seeing an obvious entrance, they walked around the building until they saw a door in a wall which they opened into a yard with a number of building entrances. The first they tried led into the children's toilets. The second led them into the middle of an infant's class. The youngish girl teacher — a complete stranger to them — said: 'You've been in there rather a long time, haven't you?'

When Peter saw the new, glamorous, pupil teacher at the Top School, he could not forbear to quote the great thought of his old boss Fred.

'By gum ar'd raytha fayle 'er than fayle badly.'

* * * * *

Young William had been to Peter Percy's butcher's shop and had come home with a bull's pizzle. He was warming it at the fire and rubbing it and trying to blow into it. 'Wot ar yew deowing, William?' said Mrs B, 'Ar'm tryin' ter blew this bladda up fer a footba'' says William (that was then a usual toy). 'That's non a bladda, yer daft aputh', quoth Mrs B, 'That's wot yer grayse yer boots wi.'

* * * * *

Mrs Bill D's two little girls got up one morning with their bottoms covered in yellow sticky stuff. Mary, who thought they'd messed themselves, gave them a lecture not to be lazy, and a walloping. When she went upstairs later she found eggshells in their bed. Their aunt had given them a hen egg each for Easter. Saying nothing, they had taken them to bed to sit on them, thinking that by morning they would each have a real, live, Easter Chicken.

* * * * *

Sir Herbert, the sitting M.P., had addressed a meeting at the 'Top School'. Beatty had been there and was asked how it had gone. 'That man!! ay cann mek 'is maerth say ennithin!'

* * * * *

Maurice was the wealthy iron-master who lived at Chase Cliff. For several years he bought and presented Empire Day medals to the children at the local schools. His wife was making the presentations at the 'Top School' when a mother who was watching the ceremony shouted to her young son who was fooling about at the back of the room:

'Owd thi gob an' sit dahn!'

* * * * *

Bill asked his lad what he'd been doing at school. 'Way've bin doin' guzzinters Dad.' 'Well if that's th' best tha can deow at skewl, termorra tha guzzinter t' pit!'

Tradesmen's Tales

Before the coming of motor transport the village met many of its own everyday needs. In Edwardian days there was a bootmaker and a tailor on the Market Place and another tailor at Victoria House. Even in the Twenties there were two cobblers, two barbers, and three drapers in the village. There were four butchers on the Market Place, as well as a thriving Co-op on the Common, with a butcher's shop and counters for grocery, bread, confectionery and greengrocery. Now the Co-op is no more and there is only one butcher in the Parish. In the Thirties the butchers (excepting the Co-op) still killed their own animals on their own premises in the village. The grocers had flour, butter, sugar, lard, rice, treacle and many other goods delivered in bulk, and did their own 'weighing up' and packaging. A proper grocer could weigh-up a pound of rice in a sheet of paper which was folded and tucked-in so skillfully that it could be dropped on a stone floor without spilling. James Henry the grocer on the Market Place made up different blends of tea to suit the particular water supply of his customers on outlying farms.

Milk was fetched every day by the children of each family from a chosen local farm, in an enamelled can with a wire handle and a lid. They soon learned the trick of swinging the full can in a complete circle over their heads, — but sometimes there were accidents, rewarded with pain and tears! Boys could also have regular jobs as errand boys. James Henry's sons delivered groceries when not at school; one of them had to make two trips down to Crich Carr every Saturday carrying two baskets of bread and groceries to one large family. The eventual purchase of a basket-carrying bicycle was a great treat.

Before the Second World War there were at least four building contractors in Crich who employed ten or more craftsmen each, including plumbers, masons and joiners. They made their own mortar and sawed and planed their own timber to make door and window frames and other house fittings. Such businesses no longer exist in Crich.

James Henry, the journeyman grocer, had acquired two mottoes: 'Think On' and 'Never Stand' which he drilled not only into his shop assistants but also into his three sons Peter, James and John. Things were hard just after the 1926 General Strike and a grocer sold-off all sorts of odds and ends cheaply. One small boy went into the corner shop under the trees on the Market Place with two pence and asked for some broken biscuits. James, wiping his hands with invisible soap, said: 'I'm sorry, young man, but I haven't any. Would you like me to break some for you?'

* * * * *

Rake went to his front door to find a Salesman with a sewing machine. He dismissed the chap with the remark that:
'Singer's is like arse holes — evvri boddi's got wonn!'

* * * * *

Gunboat, Swifty and Mouse had a shilling between them. Swifty says: 'Annutha tanner an way cud 'ave a pint a piece.' Gunboat said: 'Layve it ter may: gie may that bob an ar'll gew an say owd Frendy.' Frendy was a Quaker and kept a shop on Fritchley Green (and members of the Society of Friends never go back on their word). Gunboat went into the shop and says: 'Hast thou got thray tanners fer a bob?' Frendy, without thinking, says: 'Aye'. As he got three sixpences out of the till he says: 'William, I'll give them to thee this time — but thou must not come again.'

* * * * *

Jack G went into Bradley's 'Clothier and Haberdasher' shop just below the Parish Room for a new hat. He was asked what size he took and he didn't know. The shopman said: 'Well, I take a six and seven eighths.' Jack replied:
'Mi 'eads bigger n' thine. Ar'd better aay an eight, nine, ten.'

* * * * *

Albert paid a shilling a week into the 'Universal Club'. After some weeks his turn came and with the pound he bought a pair of boots. They were quality. As he said:
'Them's non wokkin bewts: them's Sunday buggers.'

Lynn couldn't always afford bespoke suits. In his younger days he went to one of the well known multiple tailors for a 'ready-made'. The salesman assured him that they could provide a well-fitting suit and went to great length to measure and write down dimensions of chest, waist, hips, arms, legs etc, etc. Very impressive it was. And it was all spoilt when he disappeared into the stockroom and Lynn, wandering over, heard him call out to the storekeeper: 'George — please pass me down one of the blue medium-portlys!'

* * * * *

Peter went into Bernard's for a haircut and had some back chat with Johnny — who was in the chair — and, unusually, Johnny was feeling a bit touchy. Eventually he burst out: 'Its orr rayht fer thay! In a watch theer's big whayls an theer's little whayls. Thay may be a big whayl. But if it worna fer little whayls like may, yew big whayls ud nivva gew rahnd.'

* * * * *

Edwin was the village barber before the '39 - '45 war and for a short while after. Then for twenty or more years he worked at a hairdressers in Ripley; returning home on the bus that put him down near the Parish Room at quarter to seven. Every night, as he got off the bus, he said:
'Once more — once less' and went home to his match-stick sculpture.

* * * * *

Jack, well known for his fiery temper, ran a barber's shop in the parlour of his cottage just below the King's Arms. Dennis remembers going for a haircut and being thrown-out, unshorn, because his last hair-cut had been done by his aunt. He was told to go back and tell her to cut it properly. One day, a traveller, having a pint at the 'King's Arms', asked if he could get a trim and a shave anywhere. He was told about Jack but warned not to cross him. When his turn came he had a haircut and agreed with everything Jack said. When his face was lathered and Jack was stropping the razor Jack asked which party his customer was supporting at the coming General Election. The traveller said 'Same as you.' Jack said 'Ow dusta know who ar support — ar've sed nowt.' 'No', said the traveller, 'but you've got the razor.'

32

Jim delivered newspapers for more than a generation. He worked very hard — fetching newspapers from Ambergate Station on foot twice a day: but he wasn't always sure that the rewards matched his effort. As he said:

'Radio Times, say, onni paper thay aay. Sew, on a Thosdi: oppen th' gate, gew threw, close t'gate, walk-up t'path twenty steps, bang t'knocka, weet, hand in t'paper, gerr a hayf-a-crahn, put t'paper bag dahn, gerr aert mi poss, put 'alf-crahn in, sort out t'change, hand it oer, put th' poss in mi pocket, pick up th' paper bag, walk twenty steps dahn t'path, oppen th' gate, gew threw, close t'gate, gerr on wi mi paper rahnd. An orr fer th' profit on tew pence.'

* * * * *

He spoke on the same theme when he arrived back at his newsagent's shop after a Friday morning delivery and was presented, by his wife, with a bill from the 'Derbyshire Times' for £7 3s 9d and with his cheque book.

'Huh!! write aert a cheque — enni boddi can write aert a cheque!! Wot needs doing is ter gew up theer, deliver a Radio Times, nubbdi in: no money. Next door, Derbyshire Times, nubbdi in: more no money. Rayht dahn t' Common. Arf of 'em aert: arf of 'em paying fer a wik wi wonn an thray an ar ave ter sign a cheque fer sivven pun, thray bob and nine pennies.'

* * * * *

Eventually Jim was able to get a bicycle for collecting and delivering his newspapers. It made his life a lot easier but there was a snag: the law. As he said: 'If t' bobby stops may an sez: Bell — where's t' bell — then ar'll show 'im. T'bells theer. It's non a verri good 'un: it wunna ring: but t'bells theer, t'bells theer.'

* * * * *

Raymond was late delivering his newspapers and Mrs R wanted to know where he'd been. 'A pipe got brokken 'atween Chadwick Nick and t'Resevoy and ar've bin 'elpin 'em ter gerr on wi baggin sum a t'watta ter bring it dahn ter Fritchley fer yew.'

* * * * *

He went to the surgery to see if the Vet could deal with his cat. 'Is it a tom?' said Miss W. 'Oh no, ar've got it 'ere in me basket', was the reply.

34

She went into the tobacconists to get her husband's favourite pipeful.

'Can I have an ounce of 'Parson's Pleasure' please?'

'Do you mean 'Three Nuns'?'

* * * * *

At the Scouts Whist Drive Mrs Rn asked Guddy, the undertaker if he knew how much Jimmy Tommy had left. Guddy declared: 'Ar dunna know — when ar ay ter deal wi em it dunna matter. They orr end up t'same. Way dunna put no pockets in t'shrahds.'

* * * * *

Guddy had just lost his brother Norman, the building and undertaking business was not doing well, and he was feeling ill. Bernard asked him how he was getting on. His reply was: 'Ar've gorra bucket er trubble — an ar canna spill a drop!'

* * * * *

John instructed his apprentice Desmond to paste a sheet of expensive flock-faced wallpaper and to be very careful not to get any paste on the front. But he did. So John told him to stand still, took the sheet and wrapped it, paste side in, spirally around Desmond from head to foot. 'As a craftsman' he then pasted all over the outside to demonstrate the proper way of putting paste on the front of a sheet.

* * * * *

Syd was a highly-skilled and conscientious property repairer who — like all his kind — kept about half-a-dozen jobs going at a time, and could never promise to do a job on a particular day or complete a task by a certain date. His motto was: 'Measure twice before you cut once' and when he'd made something critical to fit in a particular place he'd lean back, look at it admiringly, and say: 'That's exactly near enough.'

* * * * *

Dennis lived in a tiny house at Dimple Hollow. There was one room upstairs, one down and a garden about the size of a couple of snooker tables. Peter saw him tramping up the Dimple swearing quietly, but steadily, to himself.

'What's up, Dennis?'
'Ar've ad ter cum aert ot'way of orr them damned coach parties an tourists dahn at t'Manse. T'bluddi butler 'as gon off boozin' wi t'head gardener an ar canna manage orr t'cakes an cups a tea on mi own as well as gie aert t'tickets in t'car park: sew, ar'm gewin ter t' King's Arms fer a bit er peace.'

*   *   *   *   *

He was a highly-skilled craftsman and his boss wanted to fetch him by car one Sunday to take him to his own house to do a tricky job. 'Can I telephone you to let you know when I can pick you up?'
'Telephone! dunna bay daft, way'n onni just on cumpney watta!'
'How can I find my way to your house?'
'Its ter complicated ter tell: just stop in Crich when yew say sumbdi wi a red nose an ask im wheer ar live.'

*   *   *   *   *

The field between Hilt's Cottages and the Dimple was always notoriously wet. The developers had a spasm of honesty when they called the cul-de-sac 'Springfield Close'. There was perpetual trouble with the drainage. On one of the many attempts to get things right Dennis looked, sympathetically, into the manhole and remarked:
'Arr, watta's narra shewda'd — it'll gew enni-where!'

*   *   *   *   *

Dennis was doing a job at Rose Cottage at Fritchley when he was invited to look at a ship's beam that had been uncovered in the sitting-room ceiling. Geoff was very pleased with his find and speculated about its age on the notion that it must have been put in when it was illegal to use new oak for civilian jobs — when all the new oak went for Nelson's navy — and the only oak that could be used for building was that from a ship-breaker's yard. 'And you can't get much further from the sea than Fritchley!' But Dennis wasn't impressed with English Oak; he said: 'yew canna season it.' To prove his point he told how, when he was apprenticed to George, he went over to Freeman's farm at Moorwood Moor with George to put up a new barn. While he was there Mrs T took George and himself into the kitchen for a drink and asked if they'd like to see the 'Queens Room'. In a very crude, stone-flagged, house with lime-washed rooms they were shown a beautiful, oak-panelled, chamber with a moulded-plaster, colour-painted ceiling which, they were told, had been prepared to receive Mary, Queen of Scots, if ever it had been possible to get her out of Wingfield Manor.

Just before the '39-'45 War the farmhouse was pulled down (!!) and George saved the oak and put it in his workshop off the Dimple. After the War, when the National Health Service was set up, Dr John Stuart asked Dennis if he could make him a desk with compartments under the top into which he could put his patient's various records. Dennis used the wood from the Queen's room and, typically, made a lovely piece of furniture. But the first Xmas afterwards, John Stuart and his family went away and turned-off the heating in the consulting room. When they returned the desk-top had warped and one corner was raised about two inches. 'So', says Dennis, 'even after 3 or 4 hundred years yew canna reckon as English Oak is seasoned: as George said, it's orr-rayht in baulk but, in t' plank, it's rammel, it's rammel!'

* * * * *

Andrew was small but, in his youth, of remarkable strength. He had been known to walk up a ladder with a six-foot stone lintel on his back. As an apprentice he was often the butt of workmen at S Brothers. After a particularly tormenting dinner time he went up to Norman and, courteous as always, said:

'Please Mr S, can ar 'ave yer permission ter 'it Mr F!'

Travellers' Tales

Until after the Second World War much local travelling was on foot. The two gangways through the village provided useful shortcuts: one from near the Dimple to Fritchley and Bullbridge; the other from the Cliff Quarry at the Town End by Chadwick Nick to Ambergate. The latter ran alongside the foot of the Tors and through the tunnel under Sandy Lane; it was frequented by courting couples and gave rise to the local term 'to go tunnelling'.

Private transport, up to the end of the First World War, generally meant the pony and trap for those who could aspire to something better than the bicycle. There was only a handful of cars in the village, even at the beginning of the Second World War.

In the Twenties the only form of daily public transport near Crich was the railway at Ambergate, which meant a walk of two miles or so at the outset, and again at the end of your journey. There was one bus a week to the market at Derby. This was a converted lorry in which passengers sat facing one another on two bench seats.

In the early Thirties a local man started a regular service, with a proper bus, from Crich Market Place to Ambergate Station. This service, timed to connect with trains, was a boon not only to pupils at Strutts, but also to people who worked in Belper or Derby. Later the Pippin Bus Company took over and ran right through to Belper. In the mid-Thirties they were bought out by the Trent Motor Traction Company, which was largely owned by the LMS Railway Company. Then the schedules were changed, and it was only rarely that buses to or from Crich conveniently matched the arrival or departure times of trains at Ambergate.

The crude weekly bus to Derby was replaced in the early Thirties by the 'My Lady Coach', which also ran a Saturday service between Crich and Ripley. The local buses are now run by the National Bus Company, and the schedules change as does the weather. A few trains a day run to Derby or Matlock from Ambergate. Not many Crich people bother to use the 'service'.

Not long after the '14 – '18 War a big effort was made in the village to raise funds and organise a savings scheme to pay for a week in Blackpool. After months of effort many families went off by train from Whatstandwell and arrived at their destination, to wonder at the Tower and the Golden Mile. On the journey, between Chinley and Manchester they played 'penny-down'; the local ragged urchins ran alongside the train shouting 'Penny-down', and the passengers tossed pennies to them. On their first morning in Blackpool, Betsey was walking along the North Pier when she met Mrs C from the Hat Factory — who was carrying a large 'bread basket' with a cloth over it. After a little gossip Betsey asked what was in the basket. 'Ar've got orr t'rest of mi clouts in theer: ar dunna trust them folk at that Boarding House'.

* * * * *

Gervase and his son, Young Garve, ran a local coal-delivery business and 'My Lady' coach-service to Derby on Market Day and from Crich to Ripley on Saturdays, at the time when Jessops' Canal ran over the road at Bullbridge and even a modest outfielder could throw a stone over railway, canal, river and roadway. There were traffic lights at each end of the 'tunnel'. Old Garve was, it was said, so colour-blind that he had to feel the lights to tell which was warm and whether he could pass. What is certain is that he collected fares as people got on to his bus and he never left the terminus at Ripley without saying: 'Has anybody paid twice?'

* * * * *

As he got older Young Garve took over the delivery of coal. When he went with his family on holiday to Skegness he used to swill out the lorry, put his three-piece-suite on it, seat the family with a tarpaulin over their knees — and drive off.

* * * * *

Peter had booked Young Garve's taxi to take his and his brother's family to Ambergate station to catch the 08.15 train. They were off on holiday to Wales and had to catch a connection at Derby. The taxi hadn't arrived at 07.30 so Peter went to knock-up Garve. He hammered on the door for some time but there was no response. So he found a ladder, put it up to Garve's bedroom window, opened it, put his head into the room and yelled 'Garve'. Three heads: Garve, his missus and one of the children popped above the sheets. There was only time to do one thing: so Garve got out his father's bus and drove his eight passengers to the station: just in time.

Billy got off the non-corridor train from Sheffield at Ambergate and was desperate, and the toilets were locked. In panic he relieved himself in the waiting room on Platform 6 — behind the big coke stove — and the foreman caught him.

'Hey — t'Station Master wunna 'ave that!'

'Orr-rayht — then share it aert amung t'porters.'

* * * * *

A committee of women went to London on a day trip. While waiting to meet their MP, George Brown, outside the Houses of Parliament, a policeman on duty says:

'Ar know wheer a lotta yew cum frum.'

'How cum', says Gertie'

'Yew cum frum wheer thay put t'pig on t'war ter lissen ter t'band!'

The bobby was from Stonebroom.

* * * * *

Old Nahum went on the chapel trip to Darley Dale and took a pigeon with him to train it to fly home. He saw nothing of it for about three weeks. Then, going to work one morning up the Tors Steps, he saw the pigeon hopping down. Nahum said:

'Nar owd lad — hast walked it?'

* * * * *

On the Butcher's Trip to Blackpool, Percy was really desperate and couldn't find a convenience. In agony he eventually went into a barber's shop and asked if he could use the lavatory. The barber asked who shaved him. Percy said: 'I shave myself.' 'Well,' said the barber, 'you know what you can do then.'

* * * * *

Franny went on the Butcher's Trip to London and lost his watch — he thought on the train. He was persuaded to write and enquire of the Station Master at St Pancras if it had been found. The reply said: 'No' — but the Station Master would 'leave no stone unturned' in his effort to find out if the watch had been left on railway property. On the trip the following year, as the Crich party emerged from St Pancras, a gang of navvies was digging-up the forecourt. Franny went up to them and said:

'It's verri gud on thi — but tha needna a bothered orr that much!'

Peter's very plain cousin from Blackpool was expected for tea and Pollie was insisting that he behave. 'Why should I — she's as ugly as sin and I don't like her.'

'She's got a nice disposition, even if she isn't very pretty.'

'Well then — she could stay at home, couldn't she!'

*   *   *   *   *

Peter was coming home from work on a crowded 'Pippin' bus. There was only one seat left — next to a nursing mother. The baby was not really interested and kept pulling its mouth away from her nipple. Angrily the woman said: 'Gerron wi it — if yew dunna, ar'll gie it ter this mester.'

*   *   *   *   *

Pliable, sometimes known as Dawbarn Bill, was out of work and standing, thirsty and broke, outside the Black Swan when a car drew up and the driver asked him the way to Baslow. It was a bit complicated and Pliable did his best, but the driver didn't look very sure. So Pliable insisted on getting into the car and showing the way. When they got to Baslow, he got out, the driver said 'Thank You' and drove off without giving him even the price of a drink — and he had to walk the 14 or 15 miles back. For some time afterwards he was known as 'Baslow Bill'. One evening he went into the Comrades Club and picked up a newspaper: he turned white. 'That's 'im wot ar tewk ter Baslow' he said. It was Rouse, the blazing-car murderer.

Publicans' Tales

In the days before the First World War, most of the pubs of Crich had already existed for centuries. They served the local community, and also met the needs of travellers using the historic high ground routes. Ted the postman composed a piece incorporating the names of the parish pubs.

Lord Nelson *stumbled into the* Canal. *He was fetched out by the* Red Lion, *who was fed by a* Shoulder of Mutton *held in the* King's Arms *while he was sitting in the shade of the* Royal Oak *watching the* Rising Sun *shining on the* Black Swan *flapping up to join the* Jovial Dutchman, *followed by a* Greyhound *and carrying a* Wheatsheaf *to the* Bull *which stands in the shade of the* Cliff.

Many of our tales were told in the King's Arms and for over sixty years the King's Arms was run by one family; towards the end of that time by the three sisters, Eva, Grace and Trudy. Although their brewery did, from time to time, make minor improvements it was the sort of pub where 'The rising damp soared to meet the falling damp'. There were no pumps. The beer was fetched, not in a jug, but pint by pint straight from the barrels in a half cellar at the side of the bar. In winter it was cold, but as Eva said, 'It's a poor belly that can't warm a drop of good ale'. And before the Mansfield Brewery went over to aluminium kegs, their beer, lovingly tended by Eva, was like nectar. Locals could tell when the Head Brewer went on holiday and would grumble that he was allowed to do so.

The customers were a varied lot, from joiners, miners, farmers and labourers to executives, lawyers, educationists and company directors It was a club of the best kind and not, certainly not, just a way of making money. A stranger at the bar had to wait to be served for however long it took the business being discussed to be completed.

The Elizabeth II Coronation Carnival and the Church Restoration Fund were but two of the activities centred at the King's Arms. Racing was another constant interest. Until so many of them disappeared in the Sixties, sports clubs and other societies, so essential in welding a community together, used to meet at the King's Arms and the other pubs, which together formed one of the foundations of the village.

Dennis — who was a 'regular' at the King's Arms turned to his wife one day as he approached the bar and said: 'Ma — wot dun yew wannt ter drink — in case way get served.'

* * * * *

Grace was behind the bar in the 'King's' one evening when a young boy from one of the large families up New Road went in and asked for some 'fags'. Grace said: 'I can't sell you cigarettes.' The reply was: 'Then fetch sum bugger as can!' Trudy was also faced with the same situation with a ten-year-old she knew. Her response was: 'I can't serve you with cigarettes, you'd get me into trouble.' This time the reply was: 'Cut out t'sex an let may ay t' fags.'

* * * * *

Charles E. W. was the new chemist and when he had been installed about a fortnight his mother came to visit. Mother-in-Law had moved into the village with Charles and his family and had already had a look around.

Although old Mrs W was very strait-laced and certainly never frequented public houses, mother-in-law persuaded her, just once, to accompany her to the King's Arms for a sherry. About a week later Charles' brother George, who lived in Wimbledon and had never before been north of Watford, also came to visit. He got off the train at Ambergate at about noon on a hot day and, having had instructions, started to walk the two miles up to Crich. By the time he'd climbed up the Hagg to Bull Bridge Hill he had a beautiful thirst and promised himself a pint at the first pub he came to. It was an uphill mile or more before he arrived at the King's Arms. He went into the cool, cool bar and before he could speak Eva greeted him with: 'Oh you are like your Mother!' It was nearly 20 minutes before he got his pint, but for the next 30 years or so, whenever he came to visit, he was one of the 'regulars'.

* * * * *

It was nearly eleven o'clock. There had been a heavy 'Brag' session in the tap-room and there was a lot of 'illegal' money on the table. Everyone had drunk up so Eva went down the half-cellar with her tray and eight pint pots to refill from the barrel. Whilst she was out of sight Sergeant G and a constable came in and stood in the shadow at the end of the bar — saying nothing. As Eva emerged from the doorway at the end of the bar she almost butted the Sergeant with the loaded tray. He said: 'Where are you going with that?' 'Down here', said Eva and returned into the cellar. And that was the end of that.

* * * * *

In the days before the fatal 'improvements' there was no car park at the King's Arms and people had to leave their cars on the road outside. There was always some grumbling from the local residents. One night, after closing time, Sergeant H went into the bar and asked everyone present to go outside with him. The thought was: 'We're all for it'. But the Sergeant shone his lamp up and down and then lead the way to his car to show the assembly a glow-worm he'd found and put on the back sill of the car. After that the parking, and the 'drinking up', for a time at least, was rather better done by the regulars.

* * * * *

One of Eva's favourite stories amongst hundreds (many of which, sadly, are lost) and which she used to tell with her apron twitching with laughter, was about the fellow who came home unexpectedly and caught his wife on the kitchen rug thrashing away with the milkman. 'What the hell — and stop it when I'm talking to you!' he was supposed to have said and Eva used to demonstate how he would stir the busy couple with his foot.

* * * * *

John, who lived down Snowdrop Valley in the 1920's was a bout drinker. He'd not touch a drop for weeks and then, for a week or ten days, he'd not go to work but spend his time drinking — steadily. Towards the end of one of these sessions he was sitting, morosely, in the King's Arms , where Eva asked him what was the matter.

'Har ham sixty-five: har ham sixtayn stonn an mah wife haccuses may hov himmorality. Heeeh! har honni wish har cud.'

* * * * *

Mick's sister-in-law, who was a very tall girl, as slim as a bean pole and with very long legs, went into the King's Arms to look for him. Bill H, a true Reptonian, said:

'That's a cut above the average.'

After one long session in the bar Puddin eventually staggered to the urinal — 'shewda's up'. Having relieved the pressure he stood there gradually becoming aware of the sound of water running from the spurge pipe. He grunted: 'Eeeeh — arn't ar pittlin' steady.'

*   *   *   *   *

The bar conversation got around to families and Flo was asked if she had any children. 'Oh no, — you see, my husband is only home at the week-ends.'

*   *   *   *   *

Dennis, went into the empty bar on a hot afternoon, and waited. Eventually he realised that Eva was in the smoke-room and went in to see her staring through the window at the Co-op Butcher's shop. He asked for a pint. 'Just a minute — I want to make sure that Syd phones the bets through before the 2.30.' So Dennis, who knew how long Eva's minutes could be, walked up to the 'Sun' and had a drink. When he got back to the King's Arms , Eva was just emerging from the cellar with his pint.

*   *   *   *   *

In her later days Eva's mother Louisa was completely deaf. She could lip-read, but she lived in a silent world. She was the nominal landlady at the King's Arms, and also looked after the family house-keeping. As Trudy said: 'We never had custard with a dessert, — always cream, absolutely always cream'. Once or twice a week Louisa would walk along the rail track from the Tor Steps to Lynam's farm at Chadwick Nick to collect the cream. Sometimes George, driving the engine Dowie with a train of lime- stone-filled waggons would happen to come up behind her. When he noticed her on the track ahead he always slowed down and followed her at a distance at a walking pace, rather than startle her or make her hurry. George was a King's Arms regular.   •

*   *   *   *   *

Bill was very tall, easy-going, well-liked and had a number of nicknames. Usually he was called Pliable — for he was quite gullible. He invented one of the early 'advertising jingles' when he was

working at Dawbarns — the local woodwork manufacturer — and it was shown at the Crich Cinema in the early 1930's. The lantern slide simply said:
'Pliable for firewood — and that's that.'

* * * * *

In the days when pubs opened at 6 a.m. Pliable kept the Wheatsheaf. One night at about 10 o'clock Wassil and Bessie (who were the No. 1 Crich Poachers) set out to look for rabbits. They got back to the Wheatsheaf at about 3 a.m. and rattled on the door till Pliable put his head out of the bedroom window. 'Wot yew wannt?' 'Tew rabbits fer a drink, Bill' 'Orr rayht — ar'll bay dahn.' He let them in and gave them a jug of ale. 'Arm' gewin' back ter bed', says Pliable. 'Yew can let yersen aert!' Mrs D had boiled a ham and left it to cool on the thrall. Wassil sniffed: 'Summat smells gud.' They got a couple of loaves from the pantry and scoffed the lot before leaving.

* * * * *

They were unloading barrels from the dray outside the Wheatsheaf and Bill was rather careless in scotching them at the top of the lane. One rolled away and hit the wall above the Weaver Brook. It split and beer ran into the brook. Dummy, who was watching, said:
'Pliable; thay'd better gew ter Charlie's farm an borra 'is crame sepparator.'

* * * * *

Pliable's great skill was at billiards. In his younger days he was easily the local champion. Always short of money he would hang around the Derwent Hotel at Whatstandwell, on his way home from work at 'Dawbarns', to get anyone on a billiard table and to bet himself to win. One day a charabanc party came in. 'Ar'll play yew orr in ton fer a pahnd a piece', says Bill, thinking of some easy money. 'Gew away', said one of the visitors, 'Way'n cum fer a ride aert frum Chesterfield an way dunna wannt ter play. If tha wannts, wayn a young lad aertside an ay'll githi a game. Insted a playin us fer a pahnd apiece, way'll orr aay ower money on 'im'. Bill counted up. Twenty quid, he thought, and he's only a lad. I can't lose. So he took the bet on. They fetched the lad in. Bill broke and that was definitely that. The lad made a 100 break. Bill had to borrow off the landlord and he was in debt trouble for months. The lad — Joe Davis — became World Billiards and Snooker champion!

47

Pliable was married twice. His first wife, Mary, reared three sons and two daughters and, trying to cope with Bill's drinking and gambling, lived in great poverty and stress. Meekly, she died in comparative youth: greatly loved and mourned by those who knew what her life had been like. After some years of pigging-it on his own, Pliable, (who was about 6′ 3″ tall in his socks) married Sally — who couldn't have been more than 4′ 10″ in height. From the beginning Sally determined and declared that she was going to be 'gaffer'. 'Tha dusna stop at t′ 'Derwent Hotel' wi thi billiards — tha cums rayht whomm frum wok.' But Bill stayed with his game on Saturday dinner time, and didn't get home till after 4 o'clock. His meal was, of course, cold. He complained and walked out of the kitchen. Sally picked up the plateful of food and hit Bill with it straight at the back of the neck. He then began to be a bit more careful.

*   *   *   *   *

When the 'Talkies' came to Crich Cinema one of the first to be shown was Al Jolson's 'Singing Fool'. Towards its end, Pliable, with tears running down his face was heard to sob:
'Dunna cry, Sally, dunna cry — it's not real'.

*   *   *   *   *

In the tap room at the Bull's Head Dummy grumbled to landlord Herbert that he'd got a drop of poor beer. 'Wot ar't thay worryin' abaht? Yown onni got hayf a pint. Ar've got a bluddi cellar full o th' muck.'

*   *   *   *   *

Pot Jack used to call in the Bulls Head on the way home from the quarry. He was always broke, begging, and ragged. One day he said to the landlord:
'Mester B, hast got an owd pair o' trousers ar cud 'ave.' Herbert's reply was quite firm. 'Pot, thay lewks as though thay orr-reddi 'as wonn — it's a new pair thay wannts.'

Dick was landlord at the Cliff Inn just after the '39 – '45 war when there was a chronic shortage of beer. One day it was acute and Dick telephoned the brewery pleading for an extra delivery because he had run out. He was told that the brewery was sorry but it couldn't let him have any more as he'd already had his quota.

'Mebbe ar've had mi quota — but wot abaht t' customers' quota?'

* * * * *

Eva and Arthur were sitting by the fire in the 'Tap Room' of the King's Arms , when Fred from Whatstandwell came in bursting with news. He'd been in the 'Wheatsheaf' at Whatstandwell when a customer had had a heart attack. There had been a rush of telephone calls and the arrival of the doctor and then of the ambulance. Eva wasn't impressed at all. 'That's nothing — don't you remember last year when old Mr A was sitting over there and died on the spot!' Arthur remarked: 'Arr — but thet wer diffrent — ay died er thost!'

Sportsmen's Tales

In the days when Crich was still a self-contained community sports and communal leisure activities flourished. Four different football teams are remembered, each based on a different pub. At one time two of these teams were playing simultaneously. The Crich Rangers team of 1932-33 won numerous local and County competitions.

The Cricket Club, founded before the First World War, was still playing until 1963, and the Annual Dance on New Year's Eve was a well-established institution. Tennis was another popular sport; in the late Twenties there were at least five courts in the village alone; now there isn't a single one in the whole parish.

For the less active there were billiards, a Reading Room (on Sandy Lane) and regular Whist Drives and Dances. The Women's Institute (formed at Fritchley in 1923) and many Church-and-Chapel based clubs and societies flourished, and happily still do. Visiting entertainment included the Fairs in April and October, when Timmy Ray brought his roundabouts, swings and booths to the Market Place and then to the 'Dutchman' Croft. Sometimes a travelling circus or a theatrical group appeared. The Calliker Theatre, in a tent in the 'King's Arms' Croft, introduced the village to the drama of Sweeny Todd and Maria Marten. The Cinema was opened in 1923.

Young people had Scouts and Guides. The first Scout Troop was started in 1924 by Captain Barker, then manager of Cliff Quarry. The Guides were also established in the Twenties, by the daughter of the local doctor. Both movements are still thriving.

A village institution which, sadly, no long exists, was the Crich United Silver Prize Band. It played at many local functions, including Carnivals, the Whit Walks and the Armistice Sunday Parades. For many years its conductor was Sam Hollingsworth, who was himself a member of the 'Besses o' the Barn' Band, and played with them on tour in Australia and America; where on one occasion they were conducted by John Philip Sousa himself.

Bill, who had a bad wry neck, used to go to work at the Wireworks, down through Chase Wood. Then Fred Snow, who had a similar wry neck started work at the Chase, and used the same path. Bill met him in the wood, glared, and shouted.

'Ar't thay mockin' may?' and rushed at him with arms flailing. Fred resisted as well as he could, crying: 'Yew bluddi fewl, of course ar'm non mockin' thi — ar wer born so!' The tale of the encounter got around, and Bill was nicknamed 'Snowy' and Fred became 'Bornso'.

Snowy was notorious as a rough centre-half. Crich Town were playing Hanging Bridge on Peter Percy's field down the Chase. Early in the match one of the Crich players was injured and had to be taken home. As play restarted Snowy said to Blucher, who was Crich captain, 'Thay'll aay ter aay ten anor.' Within 3 minutes the opposing centre-forward was being helped off the field and he didn't return. As Snowy said: 'Ar rekkon thet evened it up a bit!'

$$* \quad * \quad * \quad * \quad *$$

One of the Derby County players had been suspended 'sine-die'. The argument in the smokeroom of the Greyhound on Roe's Lane was fierce. Sammy couldn't agree with Bill. Sammy reckoned the player would never in his life appear again for the County. Bill said: 'Nowt o't sort ower Sammy: ar tell thi Sammy — it's nowt o't sort.' 'Well ar tell thi Bill, it's rayht. Thay'n signed him bluddi died ar tell thi.'

$$* \quad * \quad * \quad * \quad *$$

Manny was refereeing a football match at the Town End. There was a scuffle in the goal mouth and the ball went into the net. Manny blew his whistle and pointed to the centre spot. The defending captain went up to him yelling that there'd been no goal: the scorer had been offside.

'Lewk in next Friday's 'Derbyshire Times' ter say ef that wer a goal err not!'

$$* \quad * \quad * \quad * \quad *$$

Every few years in the Twenties and Thirties 'Young Sandow's Circus' used to come to the Dutchman croft. The first time they came — up from Whatstandwell — they had a young elephant. Wassil was working in the turnip field for Miss M when he looked up and saw the elephant on the road reach over the wall with its trunk pull a turnip and start to eat it. Wassil didn't know what it was and ran into Miss M's kitchen shouting 'Cum quick — theer's a funny beast in t'tonnip fayld. Ay's pullin tonnips up wi'is tail an shuvvin 'em up 'is arse!!'

51

Franny had taken three quick wickets against Darley Dale and Percy was umpiring: he'd twisted his ankle and wasn't playing. With a new man in, the first ball just touched and a bail fell. 'Out', says Percy. The batsman protested that the wind had blown the bail off. 'Then', says Percy, 'Bay careful t'wind dunna blow thi cap off ont' way back ter t'pavilion.'

* * * * *

Flora was 'inspecting' at the Guide Camp. It had been a cold week-end and she asked if the girls had bathed in the river. 'No', said Irene, 'But they've all washed as far up as possible and as far down as possible.'

'And what', said Flora, 'about possible?'

* * * * *

Mike was being told-off by the Patrol Leader of the Kestrels in the 1st Crich B.P. Scouts for making a poor job of a frapping on a lashed joint on a stave bridge they were building. He pleaded:

'Per'aps ar'm non verri clever — but ar can lift!'

* * * * *

Arthur went into the Smoke-Room and greeted his brother Neil. 'Ar avna sayn thi fer tew-thray wik ower Neil — ahh abaht cummin wi may ter say that new fillum abaht 'Moby Dick'?'

'Ar dunna like them sex pictures.'

'Dunna thay bay daft — its non abaht sex — its abaht whales.'

'Sorry ah! — but then ar dunna like bluddi Welshmen eetha.'

* * * * *

Dummy was new to the Town End and was having a pint at the Bulls Head. Rake was keen to give him advice. 'Nivva thay say as tha's owt gud growin' in thi garden or else it'll be gon next dee, ar'm tellin' thi.' He spoke with feeling for that year he'd not got a single prize at the show; though his vegetables had won.

In his youth Jack (Cutty) had been a well known footballer — but a real tearaway: his family attracted 'respect' from the whole village. In later years he calmed down and became not only the mushroom collecting king of the Dimple Valley, but was known as the 'Surgery-Lane Bobby' for he spent much time observing there. One Sunday morning, as Peter and Frank returned from bellringing he saluted them, affectionately, with the observation:

'Ar cud deow wi a pup off yew tew — it'd bay a rare bogger.'

* * * * *

He was a keen allotment-holder and one of his favourite tricks, if there was a youngster near in view, was to drop a half-crown on to his boot and pretend to kick it up. Many a lad had dug eagerly looking for more coins but, although Cutty's plot got an extra bit of turnover, no other half-crowns were ever found.

* * * * *

His wife was a real scold and known to be so. When Jack told a group on the allotments that he was off back for his dinner Bill said:

'Wot is it terday then, Cutty? Hot tongue agen?'

* * * * *

In his early manhood Skimps was a magnificent goalkeeper and was spotted at a match at Wirksworth by a 'Derby County' coach. He was invited down to the Baseball Ground for a trial. Amongst others Steve Bloomer, then in his prime, tested him out. Steve said he was the best goalie he'd seen in years. But Skimps wasn't offered a place — he was 3" below the 'regulation height' for a goalkeeper!

* * * * *

In his younger days Wammy was a keen sportsman and would play for anyone who was short in the team. He played centre-forward for Wheatcroft against Bonsall in the 'Derbyshire Medals' and it was a key match. The spectators were excited and instructive. 'Put it theer'. Pass it ter Pont'. 'Shuv it o'er 'ere'. Wammy got fed up with the shouting and carrying on so he turned around and banged the ball into his own net and yelled: 'Is that wheer yew wannt it?' Bonsall won 1:0.

For many years Wammy was a member of the village band and did his share of collecting money for the 'Ambergate, Crich, Bull-Bridge and Fritchley Gas Light and Coke Company Silver Prize Band Uniform and Instrument Restoration Fund'. The Fund grew, and the re-equipped band became the Crich United Silver Prize Band, and practised every Sunday morning in the Parish Room — accompanied by the smell of roast beef and Yorkshire Pudding from the cottages on Surgery Lane.

They eventually went to Belle Vue to the Band Contest. As Wammy said when they got back:

'Way wer doin' ivva sew well till Drummer K spoilt evvrithin be playin' tew fly-shits, and lost us t'contest.'

Bellringers' Tales

A very considerable part of the lives of the people of Crich in the first half of this century revolved around Church and Chapel. The more pious villagers amongst the 3,000 or so inhabitants hoped that the eleven places of worship would off-set the influence of the eighteen public houses in the Parish, with regular Sunday services, seasonal festivals and such occasions as the Sunday School processions on Whit Monday and the Chapel Sermons. At least, the singing and the general turn-out of the different choirs and congregations were the subject of critical local debate, — even in the tap-room!

The bells of St. Mary's Church date from 1928, but are cast from earlier bells, the first recorded having been made in 1583.

As an example of the traditional ribaldry of bell-ringers, there is the current custom at Crich for the ringers to run a book on whether the bride is justified in having a white wedding, and if not, how long it will be before her baby is born.

A present practice when ringing at a wedding is to 'fire', that is, to ring all the bells together twelve times as the bride and groom emerge from the Church porch; and again a few minutes later, usually as the photographs are being taken. This can alarm inexperienced photographers, and perhaps explains why so many fail to notice that they are including, next to the bride's head, the words inscribed on a nearly memorial 'Be ye also ready'.

Arthur was organist and choirmaster at the Church in the days before the organ was electrically blown, and old Edgar pumped the bellows. One weeknight, as the choir was leaving, Edgar said: 'Well, Mr P, way 'ad a good practice ter nayht didna way?' Arthur was withering. 'We, what do you mean by we? — the choir and I had a good practice!'

Next Sunday, in the middle of the Te Deum, the organ wheezed to a stop, as the air ran out when Edgar stopped pumping. Edgar put his head out of the belfry and said:

'Well, Mr P, is it way?'

* * * * *

Mabel was the regular and faithful organist at the Baptist Chapel. One year, at the 'Sermins' and without telling her, a rather more skilled accompanist was invited to take over. But Mabel got to the organ seat first and refused to move. Her husband Leslie supported her completely. 'Yew stay wheer yew are, ower Mabel: dunna thay shift off er t'organ. Ar'll bring thi thi dinner after t'mornin service!'

* * * * *

Whenever there was a new choir boy, after his first practice, the others used to invite him to play a game of 'Choch Afire'. The new boy was taken into the church yard and, standing in the middle of a ring of the rest, was blindfolded and required to shout 'Choch Afire'. Then the others peed on him — to put the 'choch fire' out!

* * * * *

Frank had been a bell-ringer for years but his shoulder was increasingly troublesome. One Sunday he went into the belfry to say he'd have to finish ringing. Using his bad arm to demonstrate each point he said:

'Ar canna lift this arm enough ter ring. At wonn time ar cud lift it as ''igh as this — but nar ar can onni get it up ter 'ere.'

* * * * *

Betsey was in the choir and did a bit of gossiping during the sermon. Afterwards Jimmy Tommy, the local nob and church warden, remonstrated with her about her behaviour. Betsey's response was:

'Ar dunna like yew Mr L. Me mutha dunna like yew. And, wot's more, ar dunna know enni boddi as does like yew.'

A memorial at Crich Church, not noted in the Guide Books, is a simple slate tablet fixed to the outside of the south aisle. It says:

TO THE MEMORY OF
JOHN COOPER OF CRICH
who died Jan 20th 1803
AGED 56 YEARS

AND ANN HIS FIRST WIFE
who died Jan 4th 1772
AGED 28 YEARS

AND ELIZABETH HIS SECOND WIFE
who died Jan 29th 1787
AGED 30 YEARS

AND ELIZABETH HIS THIRD WIFE
who died Oct 20th 1821
AGED 64 YEARS

AND ROBERT SON OF
JOHN AND ANN COOPER
who died Oct 5th 1842
AGED 68 YEARS

Its oddity was unremarked, even by choirboys, until one day in the 1960's, when the Bellringers were sitting on a tombstone having a smoke whilst a wedding was being solemnized inside the church, Peter suddenly said: 'That fellow Robert Cooper was born two years after his mother died!'

Ike had to take the new baby to be christened because his wife was ill and couldn't go. 'Now don't forget', says Sarah, 'Sedan Abraham it has to be — after Grandpa.'

'What's the name to be?' intoned the Vicar.

'Damn', says Ike, 'Ar've fergot — tha'll aay ter call t'little bugger William!'

* * * * *

Thomas' rather tall gravestone acquired a noticeable lean so Fred, the sexton, put a wire round the top and back to a stake to stop it falling — until such time as he could do a proper repair. Philip, one dark night, was returning from the Bulls Head back to Hogg Nick through the churchyard and tripped over the wire. As he picked himself up he grumbled: 'Dammit, owd Tom owt ter 'ave sed ay wor aayin a phone put in!'

* * * * *

Mrs C went to church service and left young Sam to look after the 'sheeps head and pluck'. Pluck is sheep's heart and liver cooked in a suet pudding tied in a cloth. The instruction was: let it simmer on the fire and don't let it boil too hard. Sam was playing about and forgot his task. Suddenly he remembered and rushed to the pan where everything was one messy mosh. Sam ran to the church to his mother:

'Cum quick: shayps' 'eads etten ower pluck and roly dumplin's pulled is shot off ter fayht 'im!'

* * * * *

It was a very important occasion. For the first time, the Methodist parson was having dinner at the farmhouse after morning service. Mother had 'gone to town' batter pudding and gravy, roast beef, parsnips, carrots, potatoes, brussels and apple dumpling and custard, made with beastings, to follow. She'd insisted on all the five boys and two girls having a good scrub down and they all had on their Sunday best. Even Father was, awkwardly, wearing a tie. Mother felt that everything was going well and she was beginning to feel quite proud when Tom pushed his chair back and left the table, saying:

'Faytha — cut may annutha lump er fat. Ar'm just gewin' fer a shit!'

P's meetings in the evangelist's tent in the Dutchman Croft attracted a lot of interest in unlikely quarters. One ardent convert, who discovered a whole new world of experience, was Joe. And was he keen!! When Mr E, a local preacher who was involved in the campaign, was too ill to go to a local chapel to preach Joe volunteered to take his place. He opened his sermon: 'As many of you will know Mr E is too poorly to come here tonight: so I've come in his place as his prostitute.'

* * * * *

Muriel, the Sexton's wife, was struggling amongst the brambles in the church yard, picking blackberries, when she was heard to declare: 'Ar daht ef ar'll gerr a blackberry an apple tart aert er owd Mester Price this year!'

* * * * *

Terry was passing the Church yard with his uncle when Leonard had a coughing fit.
'Bad cough that, Leonard.'
'Yes — but there's many a bugger in there wishes he had it!'

* * * * *

When the navvies were building the 'Resevoy' up Chadwick Nick one of them died and the funeral was held at Crich Church. The coffin was carried by four navvy mates, and was led by the ganger up the church path. As they arrived the Vicar realised they were carrying the coffin into the church head first and asked the ganger to reverse it. The command was firm — and loud.
'Slew t' owd bugger round, lads!'

* * * * *

Brick had got drunk at the Butcher's Arms at Oakerthorpe and was on his way back when he suddenly felt very tired. So he went into South Wingfield churchyard and went to sleep between a couple of graves. He was awakened, suddenly, by the blower at Oakerthorpe Colliery and as he rubbed his eyes and peered around he mused:
'Crickey, Gabriel's callin' an ar'm t'onni wonn 'ere from Crich.'

One Saturday night, Brick walked, as he often did, across Wingfield Park to the Dog Inn at Pentrich. There, one of the locals was saying how eerie it was in the church yard in the light of the moon. Brick declared 'Theer's nowt in that — ar gew nearly evvri Setdi nayht thru theer an ar nivva say owt.' Two of the listeners got round the landlady to lend them a couple of white sheets, and went off just before turning-out time. Brick went plodding through the church yard on his way home. He heard voices and looked around to see the couple with sheets over them and with flour on their faces scratching at a grave and moaning, hoping to scare him. But he went over and said: 'Wot's up wi yew?'

'Way canna gerr in', they whined. Brick bashed their heads together and said:

'Yew an no bisness aert.'

Callers' Tales

The most regular caller to houses in Crich was, of course, the postman, who, as in most villages, came to know everything that was going on. Another visitor was the doctor, whose calls were noted by the neighbours with great interest and speculation, as they usually meant a vital alteration in the make-up of the community — a birth, an accident or illness, or a death. Other visitors, regular or occasional, were connected with everyday amenities of the village, — water, sewage, gas, electricity — and the Council or other authority which provided them.

Crich was always blessed with a good supply of clean water. The Holywell pump supplied the mound on which the Church is built, and there were public pumps on Dimple Green, on Sun Lane and at the top of Snowdrop Valley. Many houses had their own private pumps too, in the kitchens, still in use in the Twenties. Piped water was laid on in Crich in 1906, and the gas arrived in 1910, supplied by the Ambergate, Crich, Bullbridge and Fritchley Gas Company. Street oil lamps were replaced by gas lighting in 1921. Main sewers were installed in 1924; then the earth closets (including the friendly two-seaters) and the night-soil men slowly went. Also in 1924, electricity was brought up the Common as far as the Market Place, the poles and cables hauled by teams of shire horses.

The first council houses were built in 1928, and about the same time the roads were tarred. This was a great benefit to the doctor who was the pioneer motorist in Crich.

In the early Thirties the last permanent 'civic' building in the village was put up. This was the urinal on Bown's Hill — known to many of James Henry's cronies as 'Jimmy's Corner', because he was doing one of his stints as Chairman of the Parish Council when it was opened. It was said that he had chosen its site so that he would not be caught short in travelling from the King's Arms to the Jovial Dutchman.

Before he lost part of an arm whilst chopping mangels, and because there was no other work available, Ted used to help out on a local farm. One job he was given was to take a cow to be served at Joe's farm at the Cross. The bull was a young one and not quite up to his job. Joe tried two or three times to lift him on to the cow — all to no avail. A very frustrated Ted said: 'Joe, if that dozy bugger had got an eye in th'end on 'is tackle ay might say wheer ter put it!'

* * * * *

Ted got no compensation for the loss of his arm but he did eventually get the job as village postman and he knew everybody and what they were up to. His cottage, after he retired, became a 'rest centre' for the postmen from Matlock who served the village from vans. Without Ted's help the strangers wouldn't have known where half the mail was due, who was away and couldn't take in parcels, or which neighbours could stand in. He provided a real social service. At one time he kept, in his cottage, a supply of cigars for old Dr T who was not allowed to smoke in his daughter-in-law's rooms but was a great walker and used to call each day for a chat and a smoke with Ted. At birthday times — for his special customers — he used to compose a verse or two, which he pencilled on the envelope of a birthday card he was delivering. Since he retired, the Postal Service in the village has not been the same.

* * * * *

There had been jockeying for some time about who was going to have Aunt A's grandfather clock. In the end sister-in-law insisted and Ted's brother arrived to collect it. His car was an early Ford Prefect and try as they would, Ted and his brother couldn't get the clock in and close the doors. So they borrowed a drill and a hacksaw, cut a hole in the roof and stood the clock on the back seat. With it sticking out about 3 feet above roof level Ted's brother drove it off to Derby.

* * * * *

Before the days of vasectomy Pete, the teacher, used to send away for a 'gross' to be delivered under plain cover. One morning Ted went into Pete's kitchen where Janet was feeding her first daughter.

'Theer's a parcel fer thi — but it's brokken: 'ere's t'stuff'. And one by one he scattered the small envelopes at Janet's feet. As he left he said: 'Ar expect ar'll bay bringin' annutha delivery next month!'

63

Ted was late at the Club. 'Wheers tha bin?' 'Well, ar wer just cummin when that theer Mrs K cum ter borra a cup a sugar . At layst that's wot ew sed ew wannted: but ar worna 'avin any, an ar cud say orr t'kertins twitchin' so ar kept 'er aertside while ar got wot ew sed ew wer after.'

* * * * *

Shortly after the introduction of the Post Code a GPO van with a driver and Sub-Manager from Matlock drove around where Ted should have been delivering letters He was no-where to be seen. Eventually they ran him to ground up Bulling Lane where Ted had been to see a lady friend. The Manager handed him a letter simply addressed 'Nick'. DE4 5BQ' asked him who it might belong to and what the hell was he doing off his round? 'Eeesy: that's fer Nick D — his faytha allus send him fost-dee covers frum London. An mind thi own bisniss abaht wheer ar am. Ar deliver mi letters an ar cud a delivered this'n wi'out thee joy-ridin. If tha sez owt abaht may ar'll let on ter George Brown (the local MP who was Foreign Secretary) abaht wot it cost ter send thee tourin' rahn'd t'countryside.'

* * * * *

For years Ted used to stop on his round, every morning at about eight o'clock, at Peter's house on the Dimple, for a cup of tea. One day Peter looked up the yard and saw a stranger standing near the gate in the rain — and it was silin' down. 'Who's that Ted? Anyone to do with you?'

'Oh arr: ay's t'time an motion chap frum Matlock who's gewin wi may on mi rahnd ter say if ar've got t'rayht wok lewd'.

'Shall I ask him in out of the rain for a cup of tea?'

'Dunna thay bother — ler'm weet theer till ar've finished an ar'm reddi. It'll deow im gud!'

Years later, when Ted retired and there was a public presentation made to him in the Parish Room, the principal speech was made by that same 'time and motion' chap — now promoted to the top of the tree at Matlock.

When he was very young Ted had spent a lot of time with Grandma and Grandpa who lived at the end of Prospect Terrace in the days when the Primitive Methodist Chapel was in its hey-day. In due course it was their turn to entertain the preacher after morning service and Grandma, who was very proud of her elderflower wine, pressed a glass on to him, rather expecting praise. But no comment was made. In the end she could stand it no longer and asked him if he'd liked the wine. 'Well', he said, 'Not a lot — as a matter of fact I thought it was rather watery.' And indeed it was: for Grandpa, for weeks, had been sampling and topping it up with water.

*　*　*　*　*

Jack, who lived at Ambergate, had the Fritchley post round. He knew and was known by everybody and he knew about everybody. As he said: postcards were meant for postmen to read. But, more than that, given a postmark and familiar handwriting, he could often guess what was in the letter. He would come around the corner of Allen Lane on to the Green and shout across to Mrs W at Rose Cottage 'Maria, get yer washin' in. Annie's cummin on th'ten o'clock train'. And so she was.

He carried stamps for sale to people who couldn't get to the Post Office and, equally outside the law, he would collect pensions for those who were housebound. Of course, everyone gave him a Xmas box and usually a drink as well, and as long as he could stand (and he was usually carried home on Xmas Eve), his thanks were:

'Yew owt ter live fer evva.'

*　*　*　*　*

John Stuart was the GP and experience had taught him that geese were not to be trusted. At one particular farm, just before Xmas, he had run the gauntlet of a yard full of them. The following Sunday there was some surplus Yorkshire Pudding and instead of throwing it away he had the idea that on his next visit, on the Monday, he'd take it to divert the geese. As he arrived upstairs in the farmer's wifes' bedroom clutching his black-bag in one hand and the pudding in the other, she said: 'I didn't know that you used your little black bag to carry gravy in.'

Herbert collected rent for the Council. A long-established, time-saving, custom was to knock on the kitchen door and, without waiting, to walk in and pick-up the money which, with the rent book, was usually ready on the dresser. He had forgotten that the tenants at No 27 had changed and that the new ones were a young couple just back from their honeymoon.

As usual, he tapped on the door and walked in: he had to step over two pairs of legs sticking out of the pantry. They were indulging in the old custom of 'initiating', in turn, each room in their new home.

* * * * *

Herbert was about 50 when he said to his father 'You know, I'm getting so as I'd as soon have a pint as go to bed with the missus.' The response was: 'And I should bloody-well think so too, my lad!'

* * * * *

Joe and Nig, working for the Council, were digging a ditch. Joe, who wore a hearing aid, asked Nig how much deeper. Nig mouthed a reply but didn't actually utter a sound. Joe repeated his question and Nig, again gave a silent reply. Joe pulled-off his 'deaf aid' and threw it to the ground.

'Blast that battery: ar onni put it in last nayht — it mun bay a dud.'

* * * * *

Nobby and his fellow night-soil men had two particular sayings:

'Chuck us a lump o'thick to put mi candle in' and 'Pass ovva a bucket er thin — ar wannt ter rinse mi 'ands.' When these were quoted back at him on one occasion he got quite riled and declared: 'It's orr-rayht fer thay — it's onni shit ter thay: ter may it's bread and butter.'

When the 'Lavender Gang' from Crich were dealing with the night soil from a row of cottages on the hillside towards Holloway, where the privies were emptied from below, they occasionally found one occupied and the shouted warning: 'Theer's wonn on!' was very necessary.

When the Dimple Villas were built they had all the latest ideas: a wooden floor in the front-room, a pump at the slopstone in the kitchen, a wash-house, a separately-fired 'copper' for hot water and a two-seater with an access from the side onto the lane so that Nobby and his team could empty the night-soil without going into the yard. One morning Pollie was sharing the well-scrubbed double-seat with her sister and they were gossiping about a relative who was on the stage.

'Next month she's going to be in 'Hamlet' at the theatre in Nottingham.'

'Ooo-a, ooo-a' — and a grunt — 'That's a hard piece, Lizzie!'

* * * * *

Jack stopped on the Dimple for a word with Peter who, pointing across to Hilts Cottages, asked if the new window meant that the Butterley Company had put in a bathroom.

'Arr: t'bluddi bathrewm: wot deow ar wannt wi a bathrewm. Ar wesh evvri dee at t'pit an nar thay'n put up mi bluddi rent.'

'Surely it's better to have a closet in the house — to save going to the privvy down the garden.'

'But ar nivva use t'W.C. — ar wasna browt-up ter deow thet sort a thing in t'herse!' And he never did. But, since the Council would no longer collect night soil and it had to be got rid of, Jack used it to grow prize onions.

* * * * *

Peter was the Clerk to the Parish Council for many years and he worked for the Rural District Council. Often he would take rates down to the office at Belper. He well remembers the day when Wilf, who was 74 at the time, came to the kitchen door and said: 'Me dad's sent this.'

* * * * *

Peter and his brother Geoff and their wives were on their way to a dance at the Drill Hall at Matlock — but they weren't sure where it was. Geoff stopped the car at Matlock Green near to a seat under the trees where a couple were eating fish and chips and canoodling and asked Peter to get out and ask the way. Peter went up to the couple and said:

'Give us a chip' — which the girl did unhesitatingly. Peter said 'Thanks' and went back to the car enjoying his chip, but still ignorant of directions.

Peter visited his brother's flat, during the war, where a bathroom was shared by a female Polish doctor — who never locked the door. He went towards the toilet accompanied by a burst of Polish from the doctor's sitting room. The bathroom door — as usual — was open and he went in to find a girl-friend of the doctor lying soaking in the bath. 'What did you do' asked his brother.

'I needed a pee and I had one; I washed my hands and then I closed the door behind me on the way out.'

*   *   *   *   *

Leonard served on any Committee to which he could get elected or appointed. Not at all constructive he was, nevertheless, a sticker for accuracy in minutes and was famous for his points of order — which would hold-up business interminably. This had exasperated Peter the Parish Clerk, for years. At last, when Leonard once again stopped discussion with a point of order, Peter asked him: 'Exactly to which one do you refer?' Leonard's response was: 'It's your job to tell me which one!'

*   *   *   *   *

At the Parish meeting the discussion got around to the possibility of having a new bridge built over the stream at the bottom of Bobbin Mill Hill. It would cost ¼d on the rates. Farmer R objected:

'It's non woth it: ar cud piss oer t'watta'. Nosey, who was in the chair, said 'You're out of order Mr R'.

'Mebbe', says Farmer R, 'Ef ar wasna ar cud manage twice as far!'

Soldiers' Tales

One day in the year, the first Sunday in July, is of particular significance in Crich. It is then that a service is still held each year in memory of the men of the Sherwood Foresters who fell in the two World Wars. The service is held at the Memorial on Crich Hill, the Stand, and is attended by units of the present-day British Army, by many British Legion Branches, and by private citizens from quite a distance around. At the top of the Memorial there is a rotating lamp which at night sweeps over the countryside. It was intended that the light should shine over the homes of the fallen in both Nottinghamshire and Derbyshire.

During the early days of the First World War Belgian refugees were billeted in Victoria House; and later the attached Candlehouse was used for German prisoners of war. Under the guard of an army sergeant and his men, they worked during the day in the 'Old' quarry, inside a barbed-wire perimeter fence. One of the German prisoners was an excellent violinist, and great-grandmothers of today tell of gathering under the windows of what is now the Bakehouse to hear him play.

Crich's record in the First World War was honourable. From a population of about 1,500 males of all ages, some 390 men went on active service, (their names are recorded on a Roll of Honour in the Church) and 63 of them were killed. In the Second World War the carnage was lighter, but even so, from about the same size of population, some 22 men and one woman were killed on active service.

Ike lost a leg in the '14 – '18 war and for many years was guardian of the Sherwood Forester's War Memorial — Crich Stand. After he retired he decided he could afford to rent a colour television and was out when it was installed. When he came in and enquired what type of set it was, he was given the name of a Japanese company. He made his wife telephone the shop at Belper to fetch it back. He wasn't going to have a Japanese set in the house '- after wot thay did ter ower lads in Burma'. Somewhat later Dennis called to see Ike and a new music centre was proudly demonstrated. Dennis, who knew about the TV set, noticed it was a Grundig and asked Ike if he knew it was a German make. Ike replied 'O arr — but Jerrmans wer decent sowdgers, decent sowdgers. Wenn ar wer wounded ar wor behind theer lines an, as thay went back, wonn on 'em put a fag in me maerth, lit it, patted mi on't back an wished may gud luck afore ay ran off: bluddi sight better'n ower ambulance lot: them pinched mi watch an mi wallet when ar passed aert on mi way back ter t'dressin station.'

* * * * *

In the '14 – '18 War, Tommy, a veteran of the Boer War, was a drill sergeant with a local detachment of the 'Robin Hoods'. One day he had a squad in the 'Top-School' yard. He barked: 'Form Fowers'. Glancing down the line he saw three men standing looking lost. He yelled again at them:

'Form Fowers, yew thray — an the lot on yew — while ar'm gon ter get annutha — get yer eyes t'same road as yer feet.'

Charlie, whose blacksmith's shop was at the Cross and who was watching said:

'Ar'm sure thet's nivva rayht, Tommy, it's nivva rayht!'

But Tommy just carried on.

* * * * *

Herbert, who was called up — from a holiday at Scarborough — in the '14 – '18 war, joined a unit of the Derbyshire Yeomanry in the trenches as soon as his training was over. One chap in his section had not had home leave for 18 months and when he had a letter from his wife to say she was having a baby he was quite delighted — much to the amusement of his pals. Herbert thought he ought to have a word with him and explain things. But he was taken aback by the remark: 'Ar canna say wot all t'fuss is abaht — theer wor fower years atween may an ower Jack.'

By 1916 Herbert was a Sergeant serving in the line near Ypres. A German machine-gun post was pinning-down a platoon of the Regiment and his instructions were to skirt round the back of the post and Mills-bomb it. 'And', said the officer, 'if you succeed your name will live in history'. 'Ar'd raytha live in Bilper, playse', said Herbert.

* * * * *

After the '14 – '18 War Herbert kept the Bulls Head for a time and was closely concerned with local football. At one time he was captain of the Crich football team when they were in the final of the 'Matlock Medals'. He was riled by a number of the referee's decisions; especially the penalty which robbed him of victory. As the medals were being handed out to the victorious team he was heard to grumble: 'Thay owt ter gie t'referee a winner's medal anor.' The local Association suspended him 'sine die'.

* * * * *

At one time Herbert worked for S Brothers and was send by Norman to fit a new staircase into Hocky's house on Mill Green. As usual he made a perfect job and Hocky was delighted. He presented to Herbert — as a measure of his deep gratitude — a 2lb sugar bag full of windfall crab-apples. 'Herbert', says Hocky, 'tha't woth a cerw — these is specially fer thee — but dunna tell t'others'. Herbert, who knew Hocky's reputation as a miser, was quite 'overwhelmed' and said, somewhat tongue in cheek, 'Thank 'ee ivva ser much Mester H. It is gud on thi. Thay really mun bring Mrs H up ter ower place fer tay won dee!' Slightly, but only slightly, to Herbert's surprise, Hocky said: 'Thet's kind on thi — wheer dusta live?' Herbert reacted like lightning and insisted:
'Nivva thay mind wheer ar live — just thay cum!' — and left it at that.

* * * * *

Geoff had a chill but had gone on Home Guard duty on the Saturday night — when senna pods had been put in the tea. On the way home at about six o'clock on the Sunday morning his bowels got completely out of control — but the Home Guard Gaiters saved visible embarrassement. Corporal S, who was walking with him, remarked: 'By gum, Sam's got some powerful manure on his garden. I wish I knew where I could get some!'

Neighbours' Tales

Up to about thirty years ago the main quality of village life was its neighbourliness. It was impossible to be completely solitary; everybody knew everybody else, and you could count on your neighbours to help out if you were in difficulties, as well as taking you down a peg or two if you got too self-important.

The concern of the well-to-do of past generations for their less fortunate fellows is shown in Crich by the many private charities which exist. There are boards in the Church belfry, dating from 1774, on which are recorded: John Kirkland of Wheatcroft who in 1562 left forty shillings yearly to be paid to sixteen deserving widows forever. Edward Lowe of Plaistow in 1694 who gave five shillings to the poor forever: and the yearly rent of the Sheldon Pingle was to supply five shillings yearly; 2s 6d to the Vicar and 2s 6d to one poor widow for a Christmas Dinner.

And many other sums of money were left to the poor, down the years. In the Depression of the Thirties it was not unusual for young and old in severe money trouble to go to the Vicarage, where the Vicar would countersign a note authorising them to collect 2s 6d worth of groceries. James Henry handled many of these every year!

Neighbours also kept a check on crime, by their 'nosey-ness', and the police were part of the community. In the early part of the century there were two policemen permanently stationed in the village. They knew what was going on, and who was likely to get into trouble. Now, police in Panda Cars have to ask the villagers for directions — but a policeman has, recently, been seen walking around and talking to local people, so perhaps authority has learned a lesson.

Ruff lodged with Mrs Split (she was the one who cut the currant into two pieces — hence her nickname). He came home from work to find her papering a bedroom. She shouted downstairs: 'Thi dinner's reddi int' kitchen.' When she came down to get some more paste — which she'd made of flour and water and left near the slopstone — the bowl was empty. Ruff said: 'Asta enni more o' that puddin?' 'Yew daft bugger,' says Mrs Split, 'that wor mi wallpaper paste — thi puddin's in t'oven.'

To this day, to old timers, flourpaste is still known as 'Ruff's Hasty Puddin'.

* * * * *

Arthur's wife, Liza, kept brown ale in a teapot which was never on the hob but always on the table: she never put milk in her 'tea'!

When he was on his deathbed and everyone was being kind to him Arthur was asked if there was anything he wanted. He told Liza he'd like a bit of the ham he could smell cooking.

'Yew canna 'ave enni o' thet — it's fer t' funeral', was all he got in response.

* * * * *

When Jack (later Sir Jack) lived at the 'Mount' he was often away from home chairing a quiz for the BBC. His wife, much on her own, wanted a television set. Jack, who was well known in 'education', wouldn't buy one on the grounds that it represented 'degraded culture'. But rescue came for his wife in the form of a legacy, and she bought herself a set. One evening when Jack was at home his wife searched the garden and most of the house for him, and eventually found him, transfixed, staring at the Miss World contest on the 'box'.

* * * * *

Albert couldn't read or write. He kept himself and his wife Bertha on 7s 6d a week from Sam (for whom he worked) together with meat and potatoes which Sam also provided. Then he got the job as 'stirrer' at the sewage works at £4 a week. He and Bertha really didn't know what to do with the money: they had no family and, perforce, had developed sober and frugal habits. When Bertha died Albert got a bill from Desmond, the undertaker, for £91. He asked Pete to read it for him, and when told what it was, fetched out a tin with £700 in notes in

75

it. Eventually Pete persuaded Albert to put the rest of the money into a Building Society — both for safety and to get some interest — and was able to teach him to write his name. But Pete still needs to keep an eye on Albert and his handling of money.

Albert, because he can't read one, has no clock in the house. He depends on 'the sun'. Every Saturday he goes with Ted the Post, to the 'Comrades Club' for tombola and they are supposed to leave Ted's at about 7 o'clock. Sometimes, in winter, — or when it's cloudy — Albert gets his sun wrong and gets to Ted's a couple of hours early.

*　*　*　*　*

One winter, just after the Second World War, there were many power failures during bad weather. Mrs. C. was thoroughly fed up when there was yet another power cut.

'It's non fair! It's allus ower lights an them next door that gew aert. Lewk theer! They'm orr rayht on that theer Trent bus!'

*　*　*　*　*

Herbert James had been brought up as a gentleman and had elegant tastes. He kept a local hotel and his expenses overcame his income. He went bankrupt. When he realised he was destitute he went to the Post Office and telephoned Babington Workhouse at Belper with the message: 'Will you please reserve rooms for my wife and myself and four children for tonight and until further notice.'

*　*　*　*　*

In the 1981 census there is an entry:
'**Name** Iris V. **Born** 1893 **Occupation** Paper Girl.'

When the BBC came to interview her and go with her on her paper round in June 1981, the interviewer, who had a puffing struggle to keep up with her, asked her what her ambition was. She spat somewhat and said: 'Wot deow yew xxxxing — well think — at my age!' But this wasn't on the tape that was broadcast.

*　*　*　*　*

A neighbour caught Nobby asleep at the side of his fire in the cottage at the back of the Jovial Dutchman. The kettle, which was made of lead, had boiled dry and was beginning to melt.

'Hey-up Nobby, wek up — thi kettle is crouchin.'

77

When Blanche D was a little girl she was given, amongst presents on Christmas morning, a drum and a scent spray. As she sat down to dinner with her family and their guests, she announced:
'If you hear anything and smell anything — it's me!'

*   *   *   *   *

Tom was coming home from work and stopped for a chat with Mrs L at Tunnel Cottage. 'Wot a nice big tom cat yown got' he said. 'Arr' she says 'but ay's nivva a whomm'. 'Ar'll tek im wi mi an bring im back termorra', says Tom. He carried out the necessary operation and took the cat back: 'Ay'll non wannder off nar'. 'Oh thank yew', says Mrs L. 'How much deow ar owe yew then?' 'Nowt'. 'Oh thank yew verri much. Ar'll deow t'same fer thi summdi.'

*   *   *   *   *

Tom was being teased about being bald — but his wife stuck up for him by saying that, after all, grass doesn't grow on busy streets. Tom, perhaps ungallantly, retorted: 'Arr, ar suppose it's t'same reason as wummin dunna grow musstashes!'

*   *   *   *   *

Bill was really rather corpulent. His stomach was a real beauty — he claimed it was solid muscle. But he was always being teased about his figure and one day, fed up, he bellowed:
'Thay remember — they dunna put bay winders on shit-herses!'

*   *   *   *   *

Dougie was a proper know-all. To take him down a peg or two one of his mates decided to play a trick on him. He was down near the bridge at Whatstandwell when he was called: 'Dougie, wayn just pulled a watter otter aert o't rivva — cum an lewk'. Dougie says: 'Theers no otters in t'Darwent'. 'It's theer ont'bank', says his pal. So off stamps Dougie. 'Wheers this watter otter — ar dunna believe it'. 'Under that sack'. 'It's no otter'. 'It is'.
Dougie snatched the sack off to reveal a rusty old kettle.

Charles, the nob from Tansley, was having a drink in the 'Sun' when the talk developed into an argument about how many half-sovereigns could be put across a half-crown. None of the locals had a half sovereign, and an appeal was made to Charles to help settle the issue. He fumbled around his pockets but couldn't find any gold. Eventually and rather shamefacedly he said 'I'm sorry, I must have left my money in my other suit.'

'Arr, Mester T, that's wost er aayin tew sewts.'

* * * * *

In the 1983 General Election Peter H. and Trevor were canvassing. On one doorstep Trevor said that if there were any problems they would try and help. The man of the house said he'd like some advice and invited them in — leading through the kitchen (where a dismantled car engine took pride of place) into the back garden. This was a maze of old car tyres and bodywork, disused oil drums, and rusty iron. 'How can we help?' said the canvassers. 'Well, I need advice on how to deal with my neighbours — they're always complaining about my garden!'

* * * * *

Alan was complaining bitterly about the way his neighbours carried on. 'If you go into our bathroom and put the stool in the bath and stand on it and look down through the left of the fanlight, the things you can see are quite disgusting.'

* * * * *

Mrs B was angry about a neighbour who had been telling tales about her. She insisted' 'Dunna thay lissen ter 'er: fer evvri thray wods ew sez, ew tells fower lies.'

* * * * *

Pollie lived in a bungalow on Springfield Close and when she was over 86 years old a stranger came to the door and asked if she wanted a window-cleaning service. 'Oh no — it's only old people who want someone else to clean their windows.'

There was intense competition between Prospect Terrace, Dimple Villas, and Hilts Cottages as to who would get their washing out first on the line. One Monday morning, Mrs Joe was standing at the door, arms akimbo, when one of her neighbours asked if she was washing that day.

'Ar'd boiled, ponched, rinsed, mangled, dried, ironed, put away — and knitted a pit vest — afore nine o'clock', she said, triumphantly.

* * * * *

Ginny's husband arrived back early to say he'd been laid-off at the colliery. So she took the pan off the hob and declared: 'Orr-rayht — no wok: no taters.'

* * * * *

Terry was often held back at work and arrived home late for his dinner in the evening. On one occasion his wife, in protest, let the vegetables boil dry and brown. Thereafter whenever he was particularly late he opened the offensive, as he opened the door, by enquiring:

'Is it brown cabbage again tonight?'

* * * * *

Sisters Flora and Helen had lived together nearly all their lives and, when they were both in their seventies, Helen died. The Vicar was sympathising with Flora, who said: 'Yes I do miss her — but oh — it's so nice to be able to have a strong cup of tea!'

* * * * *

Granny was on the squab breathing her last. The family was gathered round, grimfaced, worried. Her breathing ruckled, there was a belch, and she passed on. Tom said: 'Ew's dead: t'clock's mine!'

Lovers' Tales

Many changes have been remarked on in our Prologues, but there are some things that change not at all. Old Adam has been around for a very long time; lads have always been lads, and lasses, lasses. Nowadays the media make money by talking at length, and by being explicit, and it often appears that the young are rather wicked and loose.

They may have talked less, and been better-behaved in public, but the parents and grandparents of today didn't really miss anything. They fought their battle of the young sexes as youngsters, and as they got older — as did their parents — they re-fought the battles of the older sexes. In this, the last group of tales, are set down some of those skirmishes which are remembered with a smile.

Grandpa John, one very foggy morning, was standing looking over, and relieving himself against the wall of his garden on the Dimple. In the middle of his reverie he heard a female voice say:

'It's a thick-un, Mr D'

'Arr lass,' the old boy replied, 'Theer's still a bit a length about it tew!'

* * * * *

As Grandma D said: 'Our Bill — got your Mary in the family way!! Clumsy young devil. Why onni last wik ay brok a shuvvel!

Marry your Mary? Ar shud think not! Ar'd raytha send 'im ter America!'

* * * * *

Elsie went to Peter's to book the Parish Room for a wedding reception for her daughter — who was sixteen. Peter commented that she was a bit young to be getting married, wasn't she? Elsie replied:

'Well, ew's got ter get married yew say. Still ar dunna suppose ar can blame 'er: theer's nowt else fer a young girl ter deow in Crich in th' evenins.'

* * * * *

A local preacher, who was a Deputy at Oakerthorpe Colliery, came home on Sunday afternoon to find his daughter and her young man sprawled on the sofa doing what they shouldn't do until they were married. Somehow the news got to the pit, and he had quite a bit of ribbing about his moral example and responsibilities. His reply was to declare:

'Ah well, the Lord's little lambs will play!'

* * * * *

Reg's cousin kept a boarding house at Blackpool and he arranged for Johnny and Mary to go there on their honeymoon. Both the bride and groom were strict Chapel folk and Reg arranged for two texts to be placed over their bed. He chose:

'I need thee every hour.'

'O Lord, give me strength.'

Reg's wife Olive acted as local reporter for the 'Derbyshire Times' and was ill when the village's 'Wedding of the Year' was held. Reg offered to get details for her but he was held up at work and the reception was over when he arrived. Going on to the bride's home, he made his enquiry and was told: 'I'm sorry, but you'll have to wait a bit: the bride and groom are upstairs putting their things together.'

*　*　*　*　*

It was a randy Johnny who said to his mother Mary:
'By gum Mutha — sum bugger's got ter aay it t'nayht.'

*　*　*　*　*

Benny was still a bachelor long after most of his pals had a family but, eventually, he popped the question and the day was named. He was given a lot of advice about the 'facts of life' and what to do on his honeymoon. When he went back to work afterwards he was asked quite a lot of questions about how he'd gone on. His response was simple:
'Oh it wer orr-rayht — it just fits'. A number of engineers at a local hosiery factory still refer to machine spares that are 'Benny'.

*　*　*　*　*

Perhaps it was a cynical nickname: for was not the original Little Red Hen a good little hen who never laid away from home? This Little Red Hen was always short of money and always ready to earn some. Some wives watched their husbands very carefully if they spotted Alice going for a walk along the Tors — her usual exercise ground. One of the favourite pastimes of the village youth of those days was to go 'bird' watching. As Skimps said: 'Way used ter gew pikin th' 'Little Red' En an way'd kayp quiet 'till ay'd got it in an then way'd goster an bowt.'

*　*　*　*　*

One pair, Dummy and Tommy, who had been watching, afterwards saw the Little Red Hen relieving herself behind a wall on the Tors. As she passed them Tom says: 'Wot dids't ton rahnd an lewk at it for?' Alice's reply was: 'To mek sure theer wor enough fer yew tew nosey buggers.'

Not all her 'friends' were regulars. Harry was a confirmed bachelor — with no vice. He was painting one of the big houses down the Common where the Little Red Hen then worked as a daily. Half-way through the morning she shouted to Harry to come upstairs to help her move some furniture. When he arrived in the bedroom Alice lay naked on the bed. As Harry said afterwards: 'Ew lewked fair luvly: ar've nivva tresspassed in mi life afore — but wot else cud ar deow?'

*   *   *   *   *

As Joe said to Bernard, the barber:
'Bayin' merrid's orr rayht —ew's theer win yew wannt it. Trubble is the bugger's theer win yew dunna wannt it.'

*   *   *   *   *

Mrs Joe C felt she wasn't getting quite everything that life owed her. She complained to Joe and pointed to the keenness of the rooster in the backyard. 'O arr', says Joe, 'But yew an ter remember as ay's non allus got t'same 'en to cope wi!'

*   *   *   *   *

Miss J, a prim and proper virgin, retired from teaching at the 'Bottom School'. Standing in front of her bungalow on the Common she was horrified to see one of Charley's cockerels obeying his natural instinct and chasing a pullet. The pullet dashed into the road right under the wheels of a passing car. With tears in her eyes, Miss J said:
'Oh you good little hen — death before dishonour!'

*   *   *   *   *

Donald was holding forth in the tap-room of the 'Sun' telling a joke about the Mother Superior who was questioning the young nun about how she'd got 'into trouble'. The nun described how the young man had kissed her and fondled her and put his hand on her thigh. The Mother Superior said: 'And what happened then?'
'Then, Mother, I fainted'. The Mother declared: (said Donald) 'Ah, you missed the best part!'
Old Mr B, bearded, sitting squarely on the settle by the fire was the first to respond. He grunted 'Ew'd taysted!'

Maud, every night of her last thirty years, said to her husband: 'Charlie, its nine o'clock: its time for our mintoe.'

* * * * *

Larry, who was a smallish, slight, chap, lived on 'Social Security' for years. Although he and his wife Dora co-operated well in raising a large family the rest of the time they fought like tigers. Peter, who was collecting Council House rents at the time, remembers seeing Larry leap through the glass of a door in trying to escape Dora's fury.

* * * * *

Ted the Post called with some mail. Larry was standing in the yard with a suitcase. 'Ar't gewin Larry?' Arr, ar'm gewin: ews bin on agen.' Dora came to the door. 'Ar'll githi summat ter gew wi'' she said and banged Larry with a sizeable eathernware pot. Larry went down like a log. Ted says: 'Hey-up — tha's killed 'im.'' 'Ar avna', says Dora. 'Ay's 'ad 'em 'arder'n that.' That night Larry went down the Common to Fritchley and the Shoulder of Mutton and says: 'Lewk wot that bugger did this mornin''. His hat wasn't on his head — it was on the lump.

* * * * *

P.C.Fred was having his tea one evening when there was a knock at the door of the Police Station. When Fred got to the door he found Larry there; gripping Dora's wrist. Around his neck was a picture frame with quite a lot of glass still in it. Larry declared: 'Ar wannt a sepparation frum this wumman — ew's brokken this picture oer mi 'ead an ar've browt t'evidence ter shew thi. Can tha fix it fer mi?' Fred retained his dignity as well as he could and said it wasn't a police matter, and Larry and Dora had better go and see a lawyer. They did, too. Their Solicitors exchanged letters but they kept on living together — and fighting — for many more years.

* * * * *

As Arthur said in the 'Kings Arms : 'That chap as invented them birth pills as saved many a lass frum 'avin ter get spliced. Theer wor nowt like it in ower dee. Ay oewt ter get wonn o them theer Nobelly prizes.'

Albert was caught on the Tors with Maggie, and he was married to Joan. But as Joan said when she was told:
'Dunna fuss: wot sumbdi else as 'ad ar dunna 'ave ter 'ave — an that sewt's may!'

*   *   *   *   *

When Blanche H was asked who was the father of her twins she was quite certain:
'Wonn on 'em wer Warties' and t'other'n wer Crusses.'

*   *   *   *   *

Fred, the verger, who was 70, and lived alone in a tiny cottage across from the church, came into the belfry just as the ringers finished raising the bells. Peter, having set the tenor, said: 'Just a minute' and brushed some bits off the shoulders of Fred's coat. No 7 said: 'Been in the hay-barn again, Fred?' The reply was: 'Not this mornin': mind yew, ar've plenty ter see tew, even if ar am gettin a bit tew owd'. And moving to the window of the ringing chamber and pointing he continued: 'Theer's wonn theer, annutha theer — an 'ews not even bin merrid — an t'wonn theer browt may a pie t'otha dee an sed 'Ar'm gud, yew know, ar'm evva sew gud.'

*   *   *   *   *

The young man at the head of the queue in the fish and chip shop on the Market Place looked bedraggled and utterly weary — a classic example of 'the morning after'. After a deep conversation with the older man who was doing the chips there was a long pause. Then the chipper turned and announced loudly to the whole queue:
'Yew know — ay's nockin'-off a widda at Ripley wi fower kids: theer's neow end ter th' adventuer er life!'

*   *   *   *   *

It was Saturday night, they'd been out to the Cliff Inn, and they were in bed. He was really doing his best — which was quite good — when she said, with her eyes on the ceiling: 'I can't think who it was left that cabbage on the back-door step this morning!'

Herbert went down the garden one Sunday morning to fetch a cabbage for dinner. As he bent over to cut it he had a fatal heart attack. A neighbour was sympathising with his widow and said: 'Oh ar'm sorry — wot on earth did yew deow?'

'It wer orr-rayht really — ar'd got a tin er peas in.'

* * * * *

Harold and Hilda were walking along Bowmer Lane when Hilda stopped, patted Harold's arm affectionately, and said:

'Harold; when wonn of us is tewk ar think ar'll gew an live in a bungalow at Skegness.'

* * * * *

Bill was 84 when, to a question from Peter, he replied:

'Widdas? — well ar still do mi best for 'em lad. But ar canna mek 'em smile enni more!'

89

Epilogue

Although they were relatively late in arriving, by the 1930's the real necessities of modern civilised life were available in Crich. These were piped water, mains sewerage, electric power and adequate heating. After World War II labour saving devices like vacuum cleaners, washing machines, central heating, telephones and refrigerators arrived. Later, TV and the affordable private car came within most people's reach. 'They never had it so good.'

But the Sixties also brought their causes for regret. The decade witnessed a rapid spread of the 'Coca-Cola Civilisation', and it saw the beginning of media dribble. These things, and the attraction of older children to activities at schools outside the village, contributed to the loss of so many forms of good companionship, — such as the various sports teams and the village band.

Now there are signs that many people are growing weary of allowing themselves to be bemused by 'computer-composed corn' on the radio and TV screen. Once again they seem to have learned to enjoy the local occasion. Gatherings to listen to music, to hear lectures, or to enjoy entertainments put on by primary schoolchildren, are crowded.

Let us hope, possibly with the help of the micro-chip and the fibre-optic and a new growth of 'outwork', that the time will come again when people can earn their daily bread where they live, in pleasant surroundings, avoiding the loss of time, energy and money in travelling elsewhere to work. Then a new pattern of living could arise. Then, perhaps, the spirit of T'Owd Man, the lead-miner whose ancient image can be seen in Wirksworth Church, will be abroad again.

T'Owd Man may have been ribald and lewd at times, but he worked hard, he helped his neighbours and he acknowledged the existence of things greater than himself. He also enjoyed himself in company with his fellow villagers and he had a great zest for life, — and who could want more?

Glossary for Learners and Translaters into Foreign Tongues

(a)

aay; have
aayin; having
abaht; about
aert; out
afore; before
agen; again
ahh; how
aht; out
allus; always
amung; amongst
an; and
anor; as well
annutha; another
aputh; halfpenny
apiece; each
ar; I
arahnd around
arder'n; harder than
arr; yes
arn't; am I not
ar't; are you
asta; have you
atween; between
avna; have not
awreddi; already
ay; he

(b)

barm; yeast
bathrewm; bathroom
bay; be
be; by
becoss; because
bewts; boots
bin; been
bisniss; business
bladda; bladder
bludhernd; bloodhound

bluddi; bloody
boddi; body
borra; borrow
bowd; bald
bowt; bolt
brek; break
brok; broke
brokken; broken
browt; brought

(c)

canna; can't
canst; can
canter; can you
cerw; cow
choch; church
chuck; throw
cob; throw
crame; cream
crahn; crown
cud; could
cudna; could not
cum; come
cumpney; company

(d)

dahn; down
daht; doubt
dee; day
deow; do
didna; did not
dotti; dirty
dun; do, done
dunna; do not
dunta; don't you
dusna; do not
dusta; do you

(e)

eetha; either
ef; if
enni; any
enuff; enough
er; of
err; or
etten; eaten
evva; ever
evvri; every
ew; she

(f)

fayld; field
fayle; feel
fayht; fight
faytha; father
featha; feather
fer; for
fergot; forget
fewl; fool
fillum; film
fost; first
fother; further
fower; four
frum; from

(g)

gerr; get
gerron; get on
gew; go
gewin; going
gie; give
githi; give you
gob; mouth
gon; gone
gorra; got an
goster; explosive laugh

grayse; grease
gud; good
guzzinter; goes into

(h)

han; have
hadna; had not
hast; have you
hayf; half
herse; house
hissen; himself
howd; hold

(i)

indayd; indeed
inter; into
isna; is not
ivva; ever

(k)

kayp; keep
kertins; curtains
knocka; knocker
knollin; ringing

(l)

layst; least
layht; light
layve; leave
ler; let
lewd; load
lewk; look
lissen; listen
lotta; lot of
luvli; lovely

(m)

maerth; mouth
may; me
mek; make
merrid; married
mester; Mr, man
mi; my

minnit; minute
missen; myself
mistek; mistake
moosic; music
mosh; mush
mun; must
munna; must not
musstash; moustache
mutha; mother

(n)

nar; now
narra; narrow
nay; no
nayd; need
nayht; night
ne; than
needna; need not
neow; no
nivva; never
non; not
nowt; nothing
nubbdi; nobody

(o)

oer; over
oewt; ought
on; of
onni; only
oppen; open
opperrations;
   operations
orr; all
ovva; over
owd; hold, old
ower; our
owt; anything

(p)

paynt; paint
pahnd; pound
persayve; perceive
pikin; peeping

playse; please
pleshure; pleasure
poffect; perfect
poss; purse
pun; pound

(r)

rahnd; round
rammel; rubbish
rayht; right
raytha; rather
reel; real
rekkon; reckon
reddi; ready
rivva; river

(s)

sargery; surgery
sarvice; service
say; see
sayn; seen
sed; said
sepparation; separation
sew; so
sewn; soon
sewts; suits
Setdi; Saturday
sez; says
shayp; sheep
shew; show
shewda; shoulder
shewin; showing
shonna; shall not
shot; shirt
shotta; will you
shrahds; shrouds
shud; should
shuvvel; shovel
shuvvin; shoving
silin; pouring
sin; since
sivven; seven
skewl; school

slopstewn; sink
sorry-ah indeed
sough; water channel
sowdger; soldier
squab; settee
stewn; stone
stonn; stone
stunna; stunner
sum; some
sumbdi; somebody
summat; something
summdi; someday
swallad; swallowed

(t)

tators; potatoes
tay; tea
taych; teach
taysted; tasted
tek; take
ter; to
termorra; tomorrow
tew; two, too
tewk; took
tha; you
thahsund; thousand
thay; you, they
thayn; you, they have
theer; there
thet; that

thi; you, your
Thosdi; Thursday
thost; thirst
thowt; thought
thrall; stone bench
thray; three
threw; through
ton; turn
tonnip; turnip
towd; told
trubble; trouble

(u)

ud; would
un; one

(v)

verri; very

(w)

wannt; want
wannder; wander
war; wall
wasna; was not
watta; water
way; we
wayn; we are, have
weet; wait
wek; wake
wenn; when
wer; were

wesh; wash
whayls; wheels
wheer; where
whomm; home
wi; with
widda; widow
wik; week
win; when
winder; window
wod; word
wonn; one
wok; work
wokkin; working
wor; was
worna; was not
wost; worst
wot; what
woth; worth
wud; would
wumman; woman
wunna; will not
wutta; will you

(y)

yed; head
yer; your
yersen; yourself
yew; you
yewth; youth
yor; your
yown; you have

Other Books in the Scarthin List

Hanged for a Sheep: *Crime in Bygone Derbyshire* by E. G. Power £1.95.
A factual but entertaining survey of crime in the days of stocks,
transportation and public executions.
Photographs and facsimile documents.

Journey from Darkness by Gordon Ottewell £1.95.
An exciting adventure for older children set in Victorian Derbyshire —
the main characters, a pit-boy and his pony.
Striking illustrations by Geoff Taylor.

Ancient Wells and Springs of Derbyshire by Peter J. Naylor £1.95.
The only book which surveys the natural water sources of Derbyshire and
describes their lore and traditions.
Profusely illustrated, with a gazetteer of sites.

The Peak District Quiz Book by Barbara Hall £1.50.
Test your knowledge, or challenge your friends with over 300 questions set
by an experienced Quizzer.

Derbyshire for Children by M. S. Dodds £1.20.
An attractive hand-written collection of puzzles, games, tests of observation
and other activities, all with a Derbyshire flavour.
All royalties to Derwent Valley Lions Club charities.

The Story of Holbrook by Doris Howe.
An absorbing study of a Derbyshire village, based on a lifetime's
personal research by the Deputy Head of a now-extinguished village school.

Due out Spring 1984
Driving the Clay Cross Tunnel by Cliff Williams.
A lively account of Victorian railway navvies at their risk-laden work and
their uninhibited leisure.

The Publishers welcome ideas and manuscripts from new or established authors.

Projected books should relate to Derbyshire or the adjoining areas.